Flipped Learning 3.0

The Operating System for the Future of Talent Development

Jon Bergmann
Errol St. Clair Smith

FL
Global
PUBLISHING

Flipped Learning 3.0

The Operating System for the Future of
Talent Development

Jon Bergmann and Errol St. Clair Smith

Copyright © 2017 FL Global Publishing
FL Global Publishing
Irvine, CA
www.Flglobal.org

Production Editor Susan Klint,
Copy Editors Kris Bergmann, Jeannette Bernstein
Graphic Designer Nina Nissly
Cover Design: Accretive Media

First Edition
ISBN-13: 978-0999139707

DEDICATION

This book is dedicated to the immeasurable possibilities we unleash by shifting from teaching
and training to self-directed learning.

ABOUT THE AUTHORS

 Jon Bergmann is one of the pioneers of the Flipped Learning movement and the Chief Academic Officer at Flipped Learning Worldwide. Jon is currently spearheading the global adoption of flipped learning by working with governments, schools, corporations, and education non-profits around the world. Jon is the author of eight books including the bestselling book: *Flip Your Classroom* which has been translated into 13 languages. He is the founder of the international FlipCon innovation summits which are dynamic, engaging events inspiring educators to transform their practice through Flipped Learning. Jon holds a master's degree in instructional technology, and in 2002, received the Presidential Award for Excellence in Math and Science Teaching. Jon serves on the advisory board for TED-Education.

 Errol St. Clair Smith is CEO of Flipped Learning Worldwide and the architect of the Flipped Learning Global Initiative. Over the last decade, he has worked closely with education thought leaders including five years as the executive director of the Academy of Education Arts and Sciences. In 2005, Smith led the development of online media channels for the nation's leading education associations and co-founded the BAM Education Radio Network. He continues to serve as Executive Producer at the nationwide network overseeing professional development programming for the Association of Curriculum Developers (ASCD), the American Association of School Administrators (AASA), the National Association of Elementary School Principals (NAESP), and the Association of School Business Officials (ASBO), among others. Smith worked as a corporate trainer for 14 years before moving into education media. Smith has four Emmy nominations and received an Emmy Award for informational public affairs programming in 2002.

TABLE OF CONTENTS

ACKNOWLEDGMENTS

Bravo to all of the Flipped Learning Global Initiative Research Fellows, Master Teachers and Ambassadors from around the world who are helping to support and advance the adoption of Flipped Learning. Your work and commitment are transforming education worldwide.

PREFACE

"The illiterate of the 21st century will not be those who cannot read and write, but those who cannot learn, unlearn, and relearn."

—Alvin Toffler

Pop Quiz: Most corporate trainers know about the Socratic method. True or false?

Let's go with true. But why was Socrates called the wisest man in the world?

The answer? Because he knew what he didn't know.

FAST FORWARD A COUPLE THOUSAND YEARS

Today, with a swipe and a few keystrokes, we can access virtually all the knowledge in the known world from a device that's smaller than an index card.

Best of all, when we're feeling particularly lazy, we can simply say, "Hey Siri, who the heck is Socrates anyway?" and voilà! Siri replies, "I've found something on Socrates. Do you want me to read it to you?"

Amazing—we have the smartest person in the world living in our pockets!

Yet, despite the super-human ways we can now access knowledge; it's astounding how often we still don't know what we don't know.

FIVE THINGS WE DIDN'T KNOW ABOUT FLIPPED LEARNING

Together the authors of this book have over 40 years' experience in education. One of us pioneered the Flipped Learning model, wrote eight Flipped Learning books, and traveled over 500,000 miles delivering Flipped Learning training. The other has been producing professional development content for educators for over a decade. If you were looking for two people who should have their fingers on the pulse of Flipped Learning, we were reasonable candidates.

But in 2016 we discovered that we were blind men walking around without a cane. We knew quite a bit about Flipped Learning, but we were painfully unaware of what we didn't know.

We eventually tripped over the depth and scope of our myopia. It turns out that Flipped Learning was reinventing itself right under our noses—morphing organically into something new and exciting. Once our eyes were opened, we discovered that Flipped Learning is very much like the famous perceptual illusion: when you look at it one way you see an old hag. But look at it another way, and it's a promising young girl—it's just a matter of perspective.

Sure, we both knew that "something" was going on with Flipped Learning, but here are five things we couldn't see and didn't know:

#1 Flipped Learning Is Not Static

There's a largely unspoken but widespread belief that Flipped Learning is a simple, static, instructional strategy. Watch the video at home, and come to class prepared to do something with what you've learned. What else is there to know?

This sentiment bubbles to the surface in many ways. We've long lost track of how often we hear:

> "Oh, I know all about Flipped Learning, it's when you record your lectures on video so that students can watch them at home."

> Or, "…Yes, I know all about flipped classrooms, I read Jon and Aaron's first book and attended a conference in 2010."

> Or, "…Flipped Learning? Been there, done that, read the book, saw the movie, and bought the t-shirt. I know all about it."

Often, the common theme in these and similar proclamations is that Flipped Learning is "static." For months we quietly accepted this worldview. Then we discovered that Flipped Learning is significantly more dynamic than most of us realize.

Like a raft of ducks paddling across an apparently placid pond, the frenetic dynamism of Flipped Learning is largely hidden below the surface. To see it you have to peer behind closed classroom doors, find portals into remote silos of learning, and gain access to private back-channel discussions.

Consequently, much of what's emerging in Flipped Learning does not show up on the radar screens of even the most passionate practitioners, astute observers, or enthusiastic evangelists. Then came the awakening!

The 2016 launch of the Flipped Learning Global Initiative (FLGI) gave us a new perspective on the Flipped Learning world. We got a panoramic window into how Flipped Learning is changing: where, why, and how.

Now, rarely does a week go by in which we don't discover some novel Flipped Learning life form tucked away in an obscure sector of the Flipped Learning ecosystem.

Our eyes have been opened, and we now know that the science, art, and practice of Flipped Learning are more dynamic and changing more rapidly than even the most experienced and knowledgeable Flipped Learning advocates realize. But why?

#2 Flipped Learning Is Evolving Because of Three Factors

The landscape of Flipped Learning is shifting because of three elements that reshape the field every day:

- Research
- Classroom Innovation
- New Technology

Research: The scope of research on Flipped Learning is staggering. The global research translated into new books and multiple languages is equally astounding. More importantly, researchers on the leading edge of Flipped Learning have shifted their focus away from asking if Flipped Learning works. Instead, the question they are now exploring is this: What factors make Flipped Learning work better?

Classroom Innovation: The second force driving the evolution of Flipped Learning is the endless stream of innovative ways traditional class time is being used. Teachers are doing things in classrooms that would have been unimaginable a decade ago. We'll explore some of these innovative classroom practices in later chapters.

Technology. The final factor changing Flipped Learning is technology. Technology developers are innovating, introducing, and iterating a blizzard of new features that make Flipped Learning easier to start, manage, and evaluate.

Before 2016, we saw these factors in the side view mirror. We had no idea how vastly, deeply, or quickly these forces were reshaping the Flipped Learning road ahead. We're now closely watching these three elements through the front windshield, and the vista is evolving rapidly.

#3 Flipped Learning Has Emerged As a Global Movement

Jon's book on Flipped Learning had been translated into several languages, so we knew there was "interest" in Flipped Learning outside the United States. But before we started working on FLGI, we had only a dim awareness of the global scope and energy that was swirling around Flipped Learning. By the time we launched, the geography of a dynamic global movement was clearly visible.

A reporter recently challenged us, "What makes you believe that Flipped Learning is a global movement?" Well, we replied, in the past 12 months we've participated in project discussions in China, Taiwan, Australia, New Zealand, Spain, Argentina, Switzerland, India, Uzbekistan, Croatia, Italy, Brazil, Singapore, Iceland, the United Kingdom, Japan, Nigeria, and Turkey.

#4 There Is a Rapidly Expanding Set of New Possibilities

The success of Flipped Learning is opening new possibilities and new frontiers. Flipped Learning is seeping into new fields, disciplines, and sectors, and has now found its way into the world of corporate training.

Companies and L&D professionals have been reaching out for help with deploying Flipped Learning for a couple of years. So when the opportunity to write the definitive book on flipping corporate training arrived on our doorstep and knocked, we opened the door.

#5 There Is a New Awareness Emerging About Flipped Learning

Reports, hard data, anecdotes, and news stories are streaming in from scores of countries around the globe. Flipped Learning is solving some of the most intractable problems of teaching, training, and learning. Indeed, many are realizing that Flipped Learning is not just another teaching tactic, but a meta-teaching strategy that supports all others.

Increasingly, the leading flipped practitioners are starting to recognize the differences between the original Flipped Learning model, blended learning, and the next generation, which is called Flipped Learning 3.0. The centerpiece of the next iteration of Flipped Learning can be summed up in one word: Awareness—awareness that there is a great deal more to Flipped Learning than we all thought.

WHO IS THIS BOOK FOR?

We wrote Flipped Learning 3.0 for three groups interested in learning and development.

> **Group #1:** L&D professionals who are new to Flipped Learning and want a step-by-step roadmap to start flipping their training. The book includes chapters designed to help trainers quickly learn the fundamentals, best practices, and right technologies to avoid the novice mistakes.

> **Group #2:** L&D professionals who have some experience with Flipped Learning and want to validate or update their knowledge with the latest global research and best practices.

> **Group #3:** Senior-level administrators and C-level executives who are considering implementing Flipped Learning and need to master the basics. Those in this category will quickly learn the fundamentals all business leaders need to know to select the right trainers and tools to ensure a successful implementation in their companies. We've also included a section on avoiding

costly and embarrassing technology purchasing mistakes.

HOW DID WE APPROACH THE SUBJECT?

We approached the topic of flipping corporate training from the bottom up, and the top down. There are big-picture chapters written from the 30,000-foot level and nitty, gritty, granular chapters that walk readers through the practical steps of successfully implementing Flipped Learning. We cover the why, what, when, where, and how of Flipped Learning. We cover the "now," and then we look ahead to the future.

Generally speaking, the discoveries of Flipped Learning 3.0 caused us to approach the corporate training space with humility. We worked hard to strike a balance between sharing what we know and staying open to what we would discover and learn along the way.

Writing the book was an exhilarating rocket ride that culminated with an exciting vision for the future of corporate training. We hope you'll catch the vision and enjoy the trip as much as we did.

You can share your thoughts, observations, and experiences with us and others in the online Flipping Corporate Training group at flglobal.org/community.

With that, we pass the keyboard to Jon Bergmann for Chapter 1: What Is Flipped Learning?

Let's take off!

Chapter 1

What Is Flipped Learning?

INTRODUCTION

Patty Evans, the e-learning and training manager at Yardi, a property management software company, used to spend her days on the road. She typically caught a Sunday flight out of Santa Barbara each week to lead weeklong trainings. On Friday afternoon, she caught the late flight home. Then one day at home and she was back on the road the next week. Life on the road was hard, and she thought there had to be a better way. During one of her frequent flights, she realized that much of the initial training she led on Mondays could be done with e-learning, and she began her Flipped Learning journey.

Her company had recently acquired another company, and as part of the acquisition, they inherited a Learning Management System. She partnered with the new LMS team and customized the product to suit their needs. This resulted in her offloading the Monday content. She got part of her life back, and instead of a Sunday flight, she flew out on Monday.

Later she realized that much of the Friday training time consisted of a certification exam, so she approached the LMS team and developed a certification assessment inside the platform. She was then able to catch an early Friday flight home—and a bit more of her life was recovered. As the program matured, she continued to work closely with the LMS team, and it caught the attention of the founder of the company. He called her into his office because he had heard that some great things were happening. He thought of one of their key clients and wondered if he might benefit from using the LMS with courses in their training. That one client trial led to five more the next year, 27 the next, and now their LMS has 260 clients. Patty's frustration with travel led her to Flipped Learning and has now turned into a profitable side-business for her core company.

Flipped Learning has its roots in formal education and is being widely adopted in both K-12 and higher education classrooms. In 2015, the Center for Digital Education surveyed United States higher education instructors and found that 29% of faculty were using the flipped classroom and another 27% said they planned to use it within a year.[1] Over half of the instructors plan to utilize Flipped Learning. Wow! But this question remains: Can Flipped Learning be contextualized and adapted for the corporate training space? And if so, how should it be adapted to meet the training demands of large and small businesses?

Margaret MacDonald is the lead trainer for Wella Hair Care. In her role, she is responsible for organizing training for salon stylists in the use of all Wella's products. In 2014, she realized that their training was outdated and needed to reflect modern teaching methods. She understood that if Wella could have a superior training program, hair salon stylists would be more likely to use her products instead of her competitors'. Margaret had some initial exposure to Flipped Learning and wondered if it might be just what Wella needed, and this prompted her to reach out to me.

As one of the pioneers of Flipped Learning, all of my previous work had been in the K-12 and higher education field. I had not thought much about how Flipped Learning could apply to corporate training, so when Margaret approached me, I was skeptical if Flipped Learning could, or should, make the leap.

During that call, Margaret described how Wella conducted their training. It consisted of one-day workshops where stylists sat all morning and listened to a series of presentations. The presentations were "modern" in that the expert trainers delivered Power Points with "gripping" slides. In reality, these presentations were anything but modern and fell short of an effective training program. After lunch, trainees were shown a demonstration of how to use a specific product, and then the last part of the day was reserved for stylists to practice using Wella hair products on a model. The problem was that with only one practice session, many stylists were not adequately prepared to use the products with their clients. Margaret said, "Stylists need at least two practice sessions." As the conversation continued, I realized that Flipped Learning could revolutionize Wella's training.

Since that initial conversation, Wella continues to transform their training methodology using Flipped Learning principles.

And yes, the stylists are now offered a much more hands-on approach, and they leave training sessions more ready to use Wella's products with their clients.

WHAT IS FLIPPED LEARNING?

Misconceptions about Flipped Learning abound, and there is a need to clarify what it is and what it is not. To get a deeper understanding of Flipped Learning, let's divide learning into two different "spaces": the Group Space and the Individual Space. The Group Space is defined as the face-to-face time a teacher/trainer has with her students or trainees. The Individual Space is defined as the time students spend working independently on course content.

What typically happens in a traditional classroom/training setting (the Group Space) is content delivery, also known as direct instruction or lecture. Students sit through a presentation that introduces new material. Students are then usually asked to apply and use what they learned during the Group Space time when they are alone in the Individual Space. Take for example an employee training on how to use a new piece of accounting software. Typically, an employee might attend a half-day training on how to use the software where the trainer walks employees through the tool. When the employee returns to work, they are expected to apply and use the new software. You can summarize traditional training in the chart below.

Group Space	Individual Space
Direct Instruction (Lecture): Trainer demonstrates new software.	Trainees work individually without help from the instructor. Often employees flounder and struggle with the new software.

4

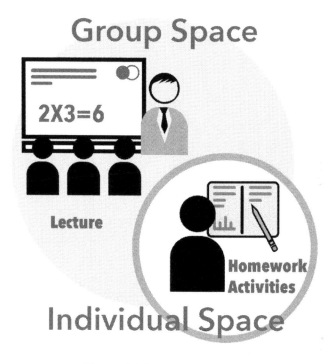

Figure 1.1 Traditional Class

In a flipped course, there is a marked difference in how the course is organized and delivered. In 2014 I, along with board members from the Flipped Learning Network, a non-profit organization I co-founded, wrote this definitive definition of Flipped Learning:

Flipped Learning is a pedagogical approach in which direct instruction moves from the group learning space to the individual learning space, and the resulting group space is transformed into a dynamic, interactive learning environment where the educator guides students as they apply concepts and engage creatively in the subject matter.[2]

In a Flipped Learning environment, the Group Space and the Individual Space are flipped. Face-to-face class time is transformed into an active place of learning.

Educational researchers have been studying learning for a very long time. In 2005, Patricia Cross wrote an article entitled, "What Do We Know About Students' Learning and How Do We Know It?" In the article, she reviewed Chickering & Gamson's Seven Principles of Good Practice (listed below), concluding that, in fact, "Active learning is the grand meta-principle"[3]—in fact, the best practice of all:

1. Good practice encourages student-teacher contact.

2. Good practice encourages cooperation among students.

3. Good practice encourages active learning.

4. Good practice gives prompt feedback.

5. Good practice emphasizes time on task.

6. Good practice communicates high expectations.

7. Good practice respects diverse talents and ways of knowing.[4]

Active learning is shorthand for "stop talking so your students can learn something." It happens when students move from passively listening to learning through doing.

Ten years of research and practice confirm that hands-on, interactive, collaborative learning trumps traditional lecture where the priority is authentic learning. Active learning is student-centric, and when done well, shifts responsibility for learning to the student. When learning is more than a matter of checking a box and moving people along, active learning is clearly superior to traditional "sit and get," passive methods.

Passive learning is not effective, and learners need to do something with what they have learned, or learning simply will not occur. This principle was recently confirmed during an interview I had with Dr. Baohui Zhang, a professor of Chemistry Education from Shaanxi Normal University in China. In our conversation, I asked, "Why does Flipped Learning work?" Dr. Zhang replied simply, "It is because students are more active in their classrooms."

If active learning is the key to learning, why do trainers spend so much time depending on trainees passively learning?

Let's return to that accounting software training. If the training were flipped, the trainee would watch a few micro-videos on how to use the tool either before class or as part of the class time (Individual Space), and then the valuable face-to-face time would be reserved for trainees to practice using the software with the trainer there to help with difficulties. We summarize this point in the chart below.

Individual Space	*Group Space*
Trainees watch a short micro-video on how to use the accounting software.	Trainees practice and apply what they learned during face-to-face time with the instructor there to help with misconceptions and difficulties.

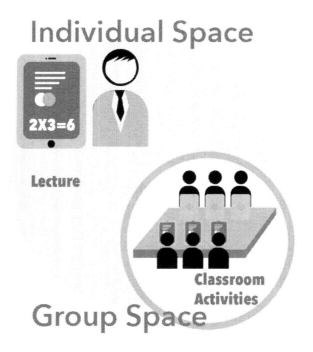

Figure 1.2 Flipped Classroom

Note that in a flipped class, the Individual Space comes first and is then followed by the Group Space. In a traditional class, the valuable Group Space is given over to content transfer, not application and analysis.

BLOOM'S TAXONOMY AND FLIPPED LEARNING

In 1956, Benjamin Bloom developed a taxonomy in which he ranked levels of cognition.[5] It was further revised by one of his students, Lauren Anderson, in 2001.[6]

The revised taxonomy is typically pictured as a pyramid.

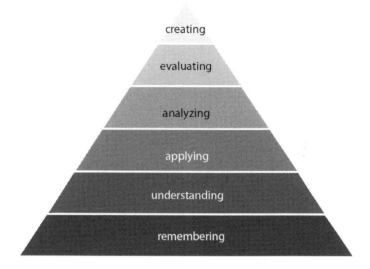

Figure 1.3 Bloom's Taxonomy (Revised)

In a traditional class, the lower parts of Bloom's Taxonomy are completed in the Group Space, and the trainees are then expected to climb their way to the top of the taxonomy by completing practice, projects, and using tools on their own time without an expert present to help. But what if we flipped Bloom's Taxonomy? More class time would be spent on the more difficult cognitive tasks—the "hard stuff"—and less class time would be spent on the easier tasks. In a flipped classroom, the information in the lower tiers of Bloom's Taxonomy is delivered creatively to trainees in the Individual Space, while the cognitively complex tasks are done during the face-to-face time (the Group Space). Thus, the "hard stuff" is done in the presence of the most valuable resource in any classroom—the expert trainer.

In the diagram below, consider the size of each area of the graph to be in direct proportion to time spent on different tasks in class. Trainees need more time working on the higher orders of Bloom's Taxonomy with their trainer present to help them with the "hard stuff."

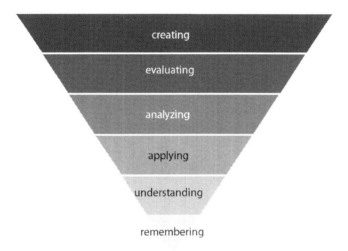

Figure 1.4 Inverted Bloom's Taxonomy

When we share the inverted Bloom's Taxonomy with corporate trainers, they are overwhelmed with the amount of time in the top two tiers of the pyramid. They don't see how their trainees can spend that amount of time evaluating and creating. And frankly, it is not appropriate or realistic in most instances.

Instead, a more realistic picture of how Flipped Learning and Bloom's Taxonomy may intersect is a diamond. Assuming again that the greater area represents a greater amount of class time devoted to the level, the bulk of class time will be used for application and analysis.

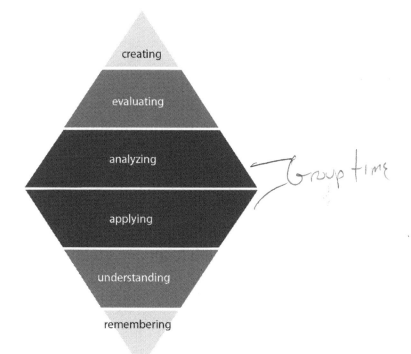

Figure 1.5 A Realistic Bloom's Taxonomy

For too long, training has been upside down about which tasks are done in the group space and what is done in the individual space. Class time should be used more thoughtfully in ways that allow all trainees to receive the support they need. In doing so, all trainees benefit. In the diamond model of Bloom's Taxonomy, flipping the class simplifies the learning process for trainees and trainers by matching the right resource (the expert trainer) to the biggest need (trainees struggling with higher-order thinking, tasks, and expectations).

THE ONE QUESTION

Anyone born before the information age grew up in an information-scarce world. To access most information, we had to search through textbooks and training manuals. We learned mostly from experts who had gone through the school of hard knocks. But now, simply by using a device in their pockets, most people have access to virtually any information. They are more likely to go to YouTube than pick up a manual. Considering this ubiquitous access to information, rethinking training is more important now than ever.

Flipped classrooms hinge on one key question: What is the best use of face-to-face training time? Or, to put it another way, what is the best use of Group Space time? This question should guide all flipped classroom design and implementation. There is no one best answer to the question, as the best use of Group Space time is dependent on the nature of the course, the content, the level expected, and many other factors. But though there are many "right" answers to this question, there is one "wrong" answer: content delivery. Too often face-to-face training time is used for disseminating information rather than creating a rich learning environment in which learners apply, analyze, and use the knowledge gained. Group Space time is best used not for content delivery, but rather for active learning.

And now I pass the keyboard over to Errol, who will take the 30,000-foot view of Flipped Learning and explore whether Flipped Learning is the right strategy for corporate training (Chapter 2), examine the unique needs of Flipped Learning in a corporate context (Chapter 3), and scope out the global reach of Flipped Learning (Chapter 4).

Chapter 2

Is Flipped Learning the Right Solution for Corporate Training?

FOLLOW THE SMART MONEY

It was Christmas Eve at the elegant home of a very successful businessman. At age 19, I was both the youngest guest and way out of my league. I had never been invited to a dinner party, tasted wine from a bottle with a cork, or received investment advice from a total stranger. But after a few sips of Chardonnay, a guest shared a tale of exceptional business savvy, offered an unsolicited recommendation, and closed by smugly saying, "Follow the smart money."

What? I had no idea what he was talking about. In my waning teenage world, money was green—it wasn't smart. Smart wasn't even an option in my adolescent universe. How could money possibly be intelligent? And even if money could think and lead, where would I follow it? A few years later I learned that the self-assured but puzzling guest was encouraging me to follow what informed, "smart people" are doing with their money. But of course, you know that. However, neither you nor I knew that this random piece of advice would become useful on the day we decided to write this book.

As Jon and I set out to explore whether Flipped Learning could be as transformational in business training as it is in education, we soon realized that we needed some smart rules of thumb to guide us.

We started with three.

RULE #1: THINK LIKE A CEO

In her book *How to Think Like a CEO*, D.A. Benton explains why every staff member in a company should learn to think as the CEO thinks:

"If you understand how the chiefs run the show, you'll avoid getting fired and get promoted more quickly."[1]

Presumably, we have your attention.

It's interesting to compare two recent lists of what drives training at companies. List one was taken from the 2016 Training Industry Report published by Training magazine. The study surveyed members from the magazine's member database. In this survey of business training professionals, the following surfaced as the top three training priorities in 2016:

1. Increasing effectiveness of training programs (33% vs. 29% the previous year)

2. Reducing cost/improving efficiency (17% vs. 19% the previous year)

3. Increasing learner usage of training programs (13% vs. 15% the previous year)[2]

Now, let's flip to a list created by the Great Place to Work Guide to Greatness. The report is an analysis of data from the Fortune 100 Best Companies to Work For. Part of the process of compiling the list is reviewing a management questionnaire from each company.

The guide notes that employee training is definitely a priority at the best companies and states that the top objectives are:

1. Designing development programs to engage and retain top talent

2. Aligning development programs with company goals

3. Building a robust leadership pipeline[3]

The differences between the two lists are subtle—subtle enough to be easily overlooked. So subtle, in fact, that there may be no meaningful distinction at all. Maybe the nuances are semantic. Maybe corporate trainers routinely take those big company objectives and translate them into sub-goals and a language that is relevant to trainers. Maybe the authors of both surveys just asked survey questions and expressed the same priorities through their own unique lenses.

But then again, maybe not.

In the discussions we held with training executives around the country, we were often struck by the apparent disconnect between their work and the company's bottom line. Admittedly we didn't come close to interviewing a statistically significant sample, but the interviews raised relevant questions to be pursued and either corroborated or refuted.

Coming from the K-12 education space, we found it natural to ask our interviewees how they are held accountable for the quality of their training. Surprisingly, the answer in most cases was crickets. More often than we expected, there was no prominent connection between training, training outcomes, and company performance among many of the L&D professionals we interviewed.

Hmm, we wondered. Is there generally a gap between corporate training and business outcomes? Is there a disconnect between the priorities of corporate trainers and the priorities of business leaders?

In our search for an answer, we stumbled across the work of Dr. William Rothwell and company, who offered a useful clue. (Thank you, Google!) Rothwell is a veteran collaborator with the Association for Talent Development (ATD) and co-author of the book *What CEOs Expect from Corporate Training*. Based on hundreds of interviews with CEOs around the United States, the book sets out to separate what trainers believe the priorities of training should be from what CEOs say they expect and want. Rothwell compared practitioners' perspectives to the responses of CEOs and found that a sizeable gap indeed exists. The gap was wide enough and significant enough that he characterized it as "depressing."[4]

The disconnect is echoed by other expert observers as well.

In an ATD article called "How CEOs Think," Christian Buss cites John Wanamaker's observation that many CEOs believe that half of their training budget is wasted. They just don't know which half.[5]

Buss goes on to note that corporate trainers and CEOs often speak a different language. According to Buss, "You can communicate how the company benefits (from training) to the CEO if you understand the way he or she thinks. The CEO's life is driven by a tyranny of numbers. This pressure comes from the company that needs to pay bills and from stockholders who want a return on their investment in the company."[6] Translation? At the end of the day, your CEO always has at least one eye-fixated on a key factor: the money.

How broadly we can generalize from these examples is unknown. What we do know is that when corporate profits drop, training is among the first departments to feel the cold, sharp edge of the knife. Ouch!

Nowhere was this more evident than during the 2008 economic downturn, when training budgets across the country took a hit. In 2009, research firm Bersin & Associates reported that the U.S. corporate training market shrank from $58.5 billion in 2007 to $56.2 billion in 2008, the greatest decline in more than ten years.[7] The drop was exceptional, but the connection between training budgets and profits is well established.

So what's the point?

Several of the L&D professionals we interviewed made it clear that the gap between training and business outcomes is no surprise to those in the training industry.

But as we approached the question of Flipped Learning for business, our first rule of thumb was that we should probably consider the view of the CEO and not just the perspectives of corporate trainers, learning and development professionals, or human resources.

Todd Tauber, vice president of Learning & Development Research at Bersin by Deloitte, agrees. "The best training programs start with business agendas,"[8] he explains in the article "How Top Companies Make the ROI Case for Employee Training" by Danielle Bullen. The focus can be either financial capital or human capital, but there seems to be broad agreement among the "smart money" types that the process of setting training priorities should include close communication between the CEO and training professionals.

Bullen also quotes David Vance, the founder of Caterpillar University. CU provides online training modules to the employees of Fortune 1000 companies.

"Vance encourages learning and development staff to have business conversations with the CEO," Bullen writes. "He recommends not pushing training, but listening openly about executive's challenges... Learning and development have no benefit unless employees can apply it to have an impact."[9]

Ah yes, impact. CEOs love impact. This is precisely why one of the founders of Flipped Learning connected with a CEO to co-author this book.

A CEO may have a much different view of the learning strategy than the head of HR . . . business leaders may be able to keep the budget more aligned with the overall business strategy," writes David Wentworth, the Principle Learning Analyst at Brandon Hall Group.[10]

But for L&D professionals there's a more practical reason for involving the C-level executives in the process. According to a McKinsey study of 1,440 respondents, "at companies where senior leaders set the training agenda, 17 percent spend between 6 percent and 10 percent of their operating budget on training and skill development, compared with the much lower 6 percent and 8 percent, respectively, who spend the same at companies where HR or business unit leaders set the agenda... Outcomes are much better when business leaders participate in the design and delivery of training programs."[11]

We realize that all learning and development staff are not in the position to engage senior leadership in strategy discussions. If you are not, it's useful to at least know and be able to make the case that you should be.

There are many questions to be explored and answered about Flipped Learning in business. It just seemed wise to make sure that the professional trainer and the CEO perspectives are both represented. In short, we decided to follow the smart money.

RULE #2: PERFORMANCE IS EVERYTHING

The sign on the wall said, "performance is everything." My client was a go-getter, a winner, a make-it-happen kind of guy. I was impressed, so impressed that I immediately went out and got a similar sign to hang in my office. There is something powerful, practical, and polarizing about the notion that "performance is everything." It presses for results, rebukes rationalizations, and rejects actions that don't have robust impact.

Over the last ten years, we've watched a parade of new ideas come and go in the K-12 education space. We've lamented silently as instructional methods generated widespread enthusiasm among educators, though they had failed to produce any measurable result. Truth be told, the culture of education has been a safe harbor for feckless ideas for over 100 years.

The culture of business is much less tolerant of ineffective ideas. Successful CEOs tend to look at the world through a pragmatic lens. There is something about facing the bottom line weekly, monthly, and quarterly that causes CEOs to pay keen attention to what works and what doesn't. Though mid-level managers may nurse pet projects, protect fiefdoms, and embrace tantalizing but impotent trends, the CEO is typically standing nearby with an ROI meter, ready to sprinkle some reality dust where needed. Training is no exception.

Efficacy in corporate training is a big deal because the money spent on corporate training is a big deal.

Stephen J. Gill, Ph.D., has over 25 years' experience in employee training and performance improvement. He is the author of The Manager's Pocket Guide to Organizational Learning and co-author of Getting More From Your Investment in Training. In a 2015 article titled "Too Much Training; Not Enough Learning," Gill makes an arresting observation: "We know from previous studies that only about 10% to 50% of learners (depending on the nature of the training and workplace environment) actually apply what they learn in training programs back on the job. If Training magazine's numbers are accurate and approximately $70 billion was spent on training programs last year, we can estimate that the industry wasted roughly between $35 billion and $63 billion on training."[12]

Wow! That's more than the GDP of over 70 countries. But wait! There's more.

Going back as far back as 1885, training professionals have known that learners forget most of the information they learn shortly after leaving the classroom. German psychologist Hermann Ebbinghaus discovered that in just a matter of days trainees could forget most of the knowledge they recently acquired.[13] Newsflash: I've been a CEO for 30 years and have spent sizable sums on staff training. I've never seen this factoid in any of the fine print in training programs. I'm going to hazard a guess that if most CEOs knew what Ebbinghaus discovered, the training industry would be a fraction of its current size.

So as we look at Flipped Learning in a business context, we want to apply the "performance is everything" rule. That way if CEOs ever find out about Ebbinghaus, we'll be able to explain how Flipped Learning stacks up against traditional staff training and other emerging methods and models.

RULE #3: PLAY WHERE THE PUCK IS GOING, BUT...

According to Training magazine's 2016 Training Industry report, 41% of staff training was conducted by a stand-and-deliver instructor in a classroom setting.[14] That number is down from 46% a year earlier. The trend is clear: alternative forms of training, such as e-learning, virtual classrooms, webcasting, social learning, and others, are gaining ground.

If you've followed the wisdom of the great corporate trainer Wayne Gretzky, you've heard him say, "A good hockey player plays where the puck is. A great hockey player plays where the puck is going to be."

If you embrace Gretzky's strategic thinking, you may be following the trend away from instructor-led training and toward e-learning. You may be positioning your company to play where it "appears" the future of corporate training is going to be. Well, as the Wizard of Oz would say, "Not so fast, not so fast."

There are strong foundational reasons why instructor-led classroom training still has a role to play in the future of corporate training (and probably always will). Salah Banna is director of Training Choice, an international training outsourcing company. In an ATD article titled "Face-to-Face Training Is Still the Better Choice over Digital Lessons," Banna makes a notable point that can be easily lost in the current trends:

"Live, instructor-led training has a long track-record of being effective and embraces in-depth interaction and discussion. Humans crave interaction, and tend to learn better in in-person environments."[15]

The sentiment is shared by Josh Bersin, the founder of Bersin by Deloitte. He cautions companies to avoid the trap of seeing e-learning as a magic bullet. Bersin advises clients to deliver 30 to 50 percent of training through the old school, face-to-face method.[16]

Banna and Bersin's views are supported by over a decade of research and practice in the K-12 education space. We'll do a deep dive into some of that material in the chapters ahead. But for now, suffice it to say that the smart money would probably finish reading this book before getting too excited about going all digital and erasing instructor salaries from your budgets.

THE STAGE IS SET

With our three smart rules of thumb in hand, we are ready to jump headfirst into the deep end of Flipped Learning for corporate training. How deep is the available knowledge? What will we find? How much of what we know from K-12 and higher education flipping applies to flipping staff training in business? What absolutely does not apply, and what cannot be known until we try?

By now most corporate trainers have heard of Flipped Learning, and some corporate trainers and companies have already begun to dip their toes into the Flipped Learning waters. ATD believes there is great potential for Flipped Learning in the business training context. So when they asked us to write the definitive book on Flipped Learning for business, we knew it was time to tackle the topic. Though we ended up dancing with a different publisher, our initial findings and growing interest confirm that Flipped Learning for business is an idea whose time has come.

THE POTENTIAL, THE PROMISE, THE POSSIBILITIES

So what can Flipped Learning do for you? Let's start by looking for clues in what Flipped Learning has done in K-12 and higher education.

Instantly Transformative

In the K-12 and higher education space, many instructional strategies, techniques, and models can take a while to produce any visible result (if ever). One of the qualities broadly reported and documented by experienced Flipped

Learning practitioners is a near immediate transformation of the classroom, the instructor, student relationships, and student learning.

Student Engagement

It's universally understood that putting information in front of students is one thing. Getting students to engage with, embrace, and think with that content is an entirely different challenge.

Traditional training, teaching, and instruction have a long reputation as sleep-inducing experiences. But Flipped Learning more powerfully engages students due to its natural reliance on active learning. If the holy grail of student engagement is getting students to make a mental and emotional investment in learning, the best way to pursue that investment is to encourage students to own their learning through hands-on, active learning methods. Flipped Learning has a proven track record of getting students not only to invest in their learning but to own it.

Increased Learning

Due to the increased time spent on application, practice, and deeper training, a flipped instruction leads to increased learning. There are research studies in K-12 and higher education which have demonstrated increased student achievement. These studies are quite compelling as to the efficacy of a flipped approach.[17] Though the level of research for Flipped Learning in the corporate context does not yet approach the vast amount of research in the context of K-12 and higher education, we expect that the same kind of results we find in formal education will be realized when flipping corporate training.

Active Learning

As we discussed in Chapter 1, active learning is the ultimate way to move students out of a passive, "sit-and-get" environment and into a space where they can learn through doing. Confirmed by both research and practice, active learning—where students become hands-on, collaborative learners instead of passive listeners—is the best way to enable students to take responsibility for their own learning. Flipped Learning, which takes class time that is traditionally spent in lecture and makes it a space for practice, analysis, and application (the higher orders of Bloom's Taxonomy), by nature prioritizes active learning and makes it the principal, not the secondary, mode of learning.

Differentiated Instruction

Any student will tell you that nothing sucks more than sitting through course content that isn't relevant to them. Perhaps the only thing more miserable is being the instructor of material that a student thinks is irrelevant.

The K-12 education community has broadly embraced the idea that a one-size-fits-all instructional model is fundamentally flawed. People are different, people's preferred learning modalities are different, and each student comes to the classroom with different levels of foundational knowledge, motivation, language skills, and learning abilities and disabilities. Flipped Learning enables widely differentiated instruction among many students in the same classroom. How cool is that?

In a flipped classroom, everyone wins. Students get what they are ready to learn when they are ready to learn it. At the same time, instructors get more time to offer personalized support to the students who need it most.

More Depth

Another result of flipping the training environment is that the training can go deeper. Instead of simply providing a basic training that saves time, companies can give deeper and richer instruction which results in a better-trained staff.

The Pause and Rewind Buttons

Those who are familiar with e-learning and blended learning already know about the value of being able to pause and rewind training. For those who don't, when Jon was developing the flipped model in his high-school classes, he had the privilege of teaching one of his daughters. One day she was watching a flipped video Jon had created, and she got up and said, "Dad, I love the flipped classroom." Jon asked her why and she said, "Because I get to pause you!" One of the simple beauties of conveying information on a flipped video is the pause and rewind buttons. And over the past decade, the value of those buttons has been verified by educators around the world.

How many times have you sat in a class and tried to absorb the content from the trainer and either struggled to keep up or were bored because you already knew the material? It seems that trainers either talk too quickly or too slowly. And sometimes, bored or overwhelmed trainees tune out during a critical moment. Pausing and rewinding videos gives trainees control over the pace of information. It allows slower learners to grasp difficult concepts and, conversely, allows faster learners to move on. Everybody learns at a different pace and when individuals have greater control of learning, everybody benefits.

It Is Modern

Let's face it, the way we access information has changed dramatically with the advent of the internet. There are websites dedicated to everything, and there is a YouTube video on virtually anything. Do you remember the days when you had to search the card catalog to find information? Now we simply ask Siri or Alexa. We live in the "YouTube" generation and Flipped Learning taps into a dynamic world of information access that wasn't available to most of us.

It Just Makes Sense

When we explain Flipped Learning to people, the overwhelming response is, "That makes sense." Everybody at one time or another has been in a class where they have gotten lost or bored or have simply given up. When they realize that Flipped Learning increases student-teacher interaction and gives them more control over the pace of learning, the vast majority of people tell us, "I wish I had learned that way." The time is now for training in the corporate world to just make sense.

The Universal Operating System

As mentioned, Flipped Learning has evolved due to research, classroom innovation, and technology. Flipped Learning practitioners on the leading edge now recognize Flipped Learning as an instructional model that supports all other models. In short, Flipped Learning is the operating system that makes all other instructional models more viable and effective.

MIGRATING FROM EDUCATION TO BUSINESS

Some of the qualities and benefits of Flipped Learning are intuitively transferable. Some examples include what experienced Flipped Learning practitioners have learned about:

- Making effective flipped videos and the ideal length, format, and level of interactivity

- The impact of localization, personalization, and culturally-infused content

- The significance of "production values" in content creation

- The difference between Flipped Learning with different age groups and generations

- Pedagogy versus andragogy

All are probably transferable to flipping in business.

But some points may not translate seamlessly into the business-training context. The ability to assign homework beyond the classroom is one of the biggest examples. In K-12 and higher education, homework is a given. In business, it may be unacceptable to assign work during an employee's off hours.

Business training is not analogous to traditional education on some points, and in many cases, will require hybrid strategies to employ Flipped Learning successfully.

THE NEXT FRONTIER

Most exciting are the new frontiers to explore. Two very exciting possibilities in the business context involve the ability of Flipped Learning to solve (or at least mitigate) the problem with learning loss. You remember that Ebbinghaus thing, right?

In K-12 education, progressive educators have moved away from the notion that "remembering everything" needs to be a priority in instruction. When all the information in the world can be accessed from a device in anyone's pocket, the ability to remember is less important than the ability to quickly retrieve information. Learning shifts from knowing all there is know about a subject to knowing where and how to get what you need to know when you need to know it.

Progressive corporate trainers are familiar with Just-In-Time Training and are innovating in some very exciting ways with this concept. On a personal note, I recently paid $1,300 to have the convertible top replaced on my car. I didn't replace the headliner and later decided I had to. Wondering if I could do it myself, I went to YouTube and searched for an instructional video. Yup! I found one, and in less than two hours I had learned the process and replaced the headliner in my car.

A more fascinating example occurred on an isolated island in the Caribbean. I was living on the island of Nevis for a time and was dropping one of my daughter's friends off at her grandparent's home. When we arrived, no one was there, the doors were locked, and she had forgotten to bring her key. I watched in awe as she went to her laptop and searched YouTube to learn how to pick a lock. After watching a video, she went to the front door and opened it. I was speechless! I had just watched a 16-year old, on a remote island, learn a locksmith's skill and successfully execute it, in less than 30 minutes. Most importantly, she got the training at the precise moment that the training became important to her. How awe-inspiring!

Do you get the impact of this? Just pause for a moment and wrap your head around this notion. Next, apply this concept to some of your training scenarios, then extrapolate the possibilities for Just-In-Time Training at your company. With a little vision, it's easy to see how JITT holds enormous promise, can be highly effective and is dramatically enhanced and supported by Flipped Learning. How?

Once you develop that library of flipped learning videos they can easily be reused as JITT tools when employees return to their work stations.

More importantly, what happens when the training objective shifts from telling trainees "what to learn" to guiding students through the process of how to learn—and apply—whatever they want to learn, at the moment they need to know it?

Finally, looking at all of this through a CEO's lens, we close with one question: What is the value of flipping corporate training from a low engagement, high priced, low retention model, to a lower priced, highly engaging, more effective model? In a word: Priceless!

Chapter 3

Flipped Learning: Embrace It? Challenge It? Ignore It?

"Nothing is more powerful than an idea whose time has come." —Victor Hugo.

You know those people who have to own the latest of everything? We're talking about the ones who camp out on city streets overnight to get a new iPhone.

We're talking about the ones who upgrade their computer operating systems, their cars, or their wardrobes as soon as they get the notice that a new version has been released. Innovation theorist Everett Rogers calls them the "early adopters": they discover a new thing, it looks good, and they jump on it. You probably know someone like that. If you haven't noticed the phenomenon, it's probably you.

But this chapter is not for those people; it's for everyone else.

This chapter is for those folks who own a cell phone that's at least one or two versions old. We're talking to those who don't upgrade most things until virtually everyone else they know has already made the leap.

THE WAY WE'VE ALWAYS DONE IT

Change in almost every area of our lives is happening so quickly that it's nice to get a break from the tyranny of progress. Sometimes it just feels good to ignore the next new thing and continue doing things the way we've been doing it.

Who wants to learn a new system, update a bunch of processes, or revise an entire training program? After all, it took a long time and a lot of work to get things to where they are right now. For some of us, there is only one really compelling reason to make a change: because everyone else has.

That's why we've decided to share with you what other people are doing with Flipped Learning all around the globe. What's happening in Flipped Learning worldwide is astounding. Even people who have been flipping instruction in the United States for a decade are clueless about how Flipped Learning has taken off beyond our borders. Flipped Learning has been transforming teaching and learning from Iceland to India, Spain to China, Australia to Dubai, and beyond. If you are not an early adopter, this is good news.

Yes, we understand that most people don't want to be "first" to try a new thing. Paradoxically, most don't want to be "last" either. Most of us rest safely in the middle of the bell curve, where we innovate just enough to keep our jobs and get paid just enough to keep us from quitting.

Well, if you haven't already started flipping we can assure you that you're not at risk of being first. In fact, in the coming chapters, we'll share some fascinating stories and insights from the pioneers and early adopters of Flipped Learning in business.

The real goal of this chapter is to help you avoid being last in your field to get the memo; last to get the significance of Flipped Learning; and last to get on with the process of flipping your training.

Of course, if you're already seriously considering applying Flipped Learning in your corporate training program, you should probably read this chapter anyway. Why? The CEO Rule.

RISKY BUSINESS

Listening to early adopters justify why they purchased that experimental widget can be very entertaining. But if you are going to strut into the CEO's office and tell her that the company should turn its entire staff training system upside down, you are moving into either promotion or pink-slip territory. What you say next will likely impact your career path.

Role play this one with us: Your boss asks, "Why do you think that Flipped Learning is a good idea for training our staff?" What do you say?

You'll certainly want to have a better answer than, "Some guy at a dinner party said it's a great model—I think we should follow the smart money."

Let's face it: convincing the C-suite team that the "creative" new instructional model you want to try is worth the spend is no easy feat.

Of course, presenting a gaggle of statistics can be impressive to your CEO, and we're going to give you some of those too. But when a concept is fairly new to a space, the pool of available statistics is shallow. Even when ample statistics are available, statistics alone can be insufficient. Why? Because everyone (including your CEO), knows that in a post-truth world there are three kinds of lies: spin, alternative facts, and statistics.

Considering the obstacles, one of the best ways to make the case for flipping corporate training is to take a page out of every teenager's book. How does a teenager deal, for example, with parents who are convinced that a "dumb phone" is all they need? After all, it can make calls (to Mom and Dad), send text messages, and provide a means of communication in an emergency. The teen in pursuit of a smart phone—or any other hot new technology development—would close the deal by demonstrating to their parents that "everybody is doing it"; their peers are all in possession of said tech, and besides, a smart phone is endlessly useful for educational apps in their classes, doing research for homework on-the-go, and keeping track of their practice, game, rehearsal, or concert schedules. Mom and Dad might still be reluctant, but most parents would be willing to step up the technology for the sake of their kids' education and life skills.

It's instinctive, isn't it? There's safety in numbers. If we're wrong, at least we're all wrong together. We've been on both sides of the business decision process, and here's a deep dark secret: We're convinced that more business decisions are based on the "everyone else is doing it" argument than deep, thorough business analysis. Doubt us? Try explaining the first Internet boom, the housing bubble that led to 2008 crash, or any of the countless irrational business decisions routinely picked apart in retrospect. The truth is, what you and your C-team need to begin to consider Flipped Training is "cover."

So this is the CYA chapter. (Cover your assets, of course. What were you thinking?) This chapter is where you'll get the justification, rationalization, and political cover to propose turning your company's training program upside down. This chapter is where you'll find the information to prove that you are not a nutcase who should be escorted by security to the front door. This section is where you'll get what you'll need to tell your CEO (with a straight face) that Flipped Learning is not snake oil, blue sky, mumbo jumbo, a passing fad, the training flavor of the day, or too risky to try right now. This is your defense against any of the C-level pushback that could get your assistant promoted to your position.

Do we have your attention?

TRAINING TRENDS YOU CAN'T AFFORD TO IGNORE

To be fair, there are good reasons for your CEO to be skeptical. (Beyond that Ebbinghaus learning loss thing you've been hiding from her.)

In education, we live under the relentless oppression of the next new thing. Many educators are in the field to change the world. So periodically, we hear about some new education movement that's promising to transform learning. Don't believe us? Pack for a long trip, then google "education reform."

Just since 1984, we have been through the home-schooling, unschooling, and natural schooling movements. We've seen the restructuring movement, charter school movement, and excellence movement. There's been constructivism, the common school movement, the progressive reform era, the equity movement, the standards-based reform movement, the whole child movement, Teach for America, the Montessori Method, the Waldorf Method, online learning, No Child Left Behind, Common Core, Race to the Top, the maker movement, and the education technology movement. We could go on, but you get the point. And we haven't even touched the corporate space yet.

Corporate training has seen its share of "flavors of the day" as well. Over the last few years we've seen several articles titled with some iteration of "Training Trends You Can't Afford to Ignore."

Walk back through time and you'll stumble onto ideas like andragogy, apprenticeship, knowledge management, mentoring, coaching, a la carte training, online collaboration, develop once - use many, training departments as newsrooms, skills portfolios, net-knowledge skills, intranets, the shift from "training" to "learning," individual development plans, content management, focus on extrinsic and intrinsic incentives, gamification, personal learning, formalizing informal learning, social badging, mobile learning, immersive learning, the four Cs, business-centric learning, video-based learning, competency-based training, social learning, curation for workplace learning, virtual reality, adaptive learning, and micro learning. Again, you get the point.

As we did a deep dive into the history of teaching and learning, a couple of observations percolated to the surface.

- There's always something new coming down the pike for the early adopters to embrace, the skeptics to challenge, and the laggards to ignore.

- In the ever-evolving, competitive, marketplace of education and training ideas, it's noteworthy when any instructional model breaks through and attracts a critical mass of evangelists. These are the ideas we probably should NOT ignore.

CRITICAL MASS: FLIPPED LEARNING AT THE CROSSROADS

Sharon Boller, president of learning design firm Bottom-Line Performance, looked at training strategies that were on ATD's trending list in 1998. She noted that all are early versions of strategies that are commonly used today. She went on to surmise that it takes a decade or more for dramatic change to start to become visible. She closes with:

"...yes, trends DO matter. We need to pay attention to them. What starts as a trend—with only 1% or 2% of early adopters using a process, tool, or technology—does find its way into the mainstream. . . . Eventually, however, these early trends become the way we do things. What is novel today becomes the norm tomorrow."[1]

It's been exactly ten years since the concept of Flipped Learning was introduced in the education space. The following data, reported by the Flipped Learning Network, suggests that Flipped Learning has reached critical mass in education:

- In 2012, 48% of teachers flipped at least one lesson. By 2014, it was up to 78%.

- 96% of teachers who have flipped a lesson would recommend that method to others

- 46% of teachers researched have been teaching for more than 16 years, but are moving towards flipped classrooms

- 9 out of 10 teachers noticed a positive change in student engagement since flipping their classrooms (up 80% from 2012)

- 71% of teachers indicated that their students' grades have improved since implementing a flipped classroom strategy

- Of the teachers who do not flip their classroom lessons, 89% said that they would be interested in learning more about the pedagogy[2]

But wait, there's more!

Flipped Learning has reached beyond its K-12 roots and invaded learning in some unexpected places.

Higher Education

Higher education has enthusiastically embraced Flipped Learning, including prestigious universities like Harvard, MIT, and Stanford. Flipped Learning has taken root at universities in Australia, Taiwan, and China. And the first fully flipped university is currently turning higher education upside down in Istanbul, Turkey.

As two corporate trainers we interviewed noted, "college students who 'learn how to learn' in a flipped way will expect their future employers to provide training for them in those ways, just as previous generations have expected 'stand and deliver' training."

Content

The subjects being flipped span a wide spectrum, including math, science, medicine, law, engineering, physical education, dance, negotiation, civics, foreign languages, and special needs—to list a few.

We are regularly astounded to hear the tales of subjects being flipped that we had never considered.

Countries

The list of countries with accelerating interest in Flipped Learning is also jaw dropping. At the Flipped Learning Global Initiative (FLGlobal.org) we have received calls for Flipped Learning training and support from countries all over the world including:

• Taiwan	• Nigeria	• Japan
• UK	• South Africa	• France
• Chile	• Italy	• United States
• Spain	• Brazil	• New Zealand
• Norway	• Uzbekistan	• Egypt
• Sweden	• UAE	• Australia
• Switzerland	• Iceland	• Korea
• Mexico	• Argentina	• Indonesia
• Singapore	• China	• Croatia

In several countries, there are high-level efforts underway to introduce Flipped Learning into the education system. Hot spots around the globe include: Singapore: Nanyang

Technological University (NTU) spent $75 million to implement the flipped classroom model.

Spain: The Ministry of Education has sponsored a Flipped Learning Conference Iceland: 20–25% of the teachers are flipping, and adoption is rapidly expanding. Italy: A textbook publisher is training 100 teachers a week in Flipped Learning. Taiwan and China: Two multinational companies have launched ventures to flip schools in the country. Argentina: The Ministry of Education is working to flip the entire province of Misiones. Australia: Flipped Learning has been nationally recognized, and the country currently has the most Flipped Learning Certified Teachers.

Social Media

Online there are Flipped Learning social networks with thousands of users in the US, Korea, Italy, Sweden, Japan and Hong Kong.

Evangelists

The Flipped Learning Global Initiative now has Research Fellows, and Master Teachers from ten countries and more than 50 Flipped Learning Ambassadors on six continents.

Now let's switch perspectives and look at Flipped Learning through a lens that your CEO will appreciate.

SHOW ME THE MONEY

Flipped Learning was a $494.6 million dollar industry in 2015. Analysts at RnR Market Research forecast that the global Flipped Learning market will reach $2.4 billion in just three years. Growth is comprised of demand for services, software, and hardware with a projected CAGR of 37.47%. Services (which includes training) is projected to be the fastest growth sector.[3]

What's the major driver of this growth? The key drivers, according to the study, are the trends toward personalized learning and a change in the focus from classroom delivery to student learning outcomes.

The verdict is in. Flipped Learning is not snake oil, blue sky, mumbo jumbo, a passing fad, or the training flavor of the day. Smart, informed, experienced educators, professors, administrators and, yes, corporate trainers all around the globe are flipping their instruction.

Demand for Flipped Learning services, tools, and support is creating an industry that would rival the GDP of many small nations. The numbers in play speak to the global energy and interest around Flipped Learning. The projected market growth underscores that Flipped Learning has already reached critical mass as an instructional method.

All of the data points to the conclusion that motivated us to write this book. Flipped Learning is ready for the next frontier: Flipped Training for business.

ARE YOU READY FOR FLIPPED LEARNING?

One of the barriers that often deters people from embracing new instructional models is relationships; specifically, the relationship between the new model and the old.

Consider this: The evolution of teaching and learning is marked by high-stakes battles between education philosophies. Often new education models were rightly viewed as an existential threat to the old model. Those in favor of classical education had to lock horns with progressives. The champions of a secular education were fundamentally at war with religious-based schools. Even today, those who favor a unified national education policy and federally supported public schools are lawyering up against the state-rights and school choice bunch.

Perhaps the reason why Flipped Learning has survived, thrived, and continues to grow is that it plays nice with all other instructional models.

One of the most fascinating qualities about Flipped Learning is that it is largely pluralistic.

To test this proposition, we played a game. We made a list of the dominant education philosophies and instructional strategies from Plato to present day. Then we tried to identify the ones that could not be either supported or enhanced by Flipped Learning. The list included:

Idealism	Critical theory
Realism	Perennialism
Scholasticism	Progressivism
Essentialism	Social reconstructionism
Democratic education	Critical pedagogy
Contemplative education	Project-Based Learning
Game-Based Learning	Inquiry-Based Learning
Direct Classroom Instruction	Maker movement
Classical education	Pragmatism
Unschooling	Analytic philosophy
Standards-Based Learning	Existentialist
Gamification	*Waldorf*

Strategies that play well are in bold text. Those that don't play well are in italicized text.

In two cases, Flipped Learning was either inherently at odds with or simply did not vibe with the instructional model or education philosophy. In twenty cases, Flipped Learning could potentially support and enhance them.

We also looked at the latest corporate training models: Gamification, personal learning, social learning, formalizing informal learning, mobile learning, immersive learning, the four Cs, business-centric learning, video-based learning, curation for workplace learning, virtual reality, adaptive learning, and micro learning. We concluded that Flipped Learning could support each of these training concepts as well.

The bottom line? You don't have to give up your pedagogical religion to embrace Flipped Learning. You can be for Flipped Learning without being against PBL, or gamification, or team-based learning, or personalization, or virtual reality, or micro-learning, or almost any instructional or training strategy. How can this be?

FRAMEWORK, FOUNDATION, FACILITATOR

With any instructional philosophy, model, or strategy, as we stated earlier, one of the pivotal questions is this: What is the best use of the teacher's or trainer's time? Time is the most valuable resource an instructor has. Correction: Time is the most valuable resource we all have. Fundamentally, Flipped Learning is a framework for rethinking how instructional time is used by both the instructor AND the learner.

It turns out that time is a pivotal element in learning. When we begin to innovate with time, new possibilities arise around how, where, and when instruction happens.

Flipped Learning allows you to shift training time in three significant ways:

- Shifting from an instructor-designated time and pace to an individual learner–determined time and pace

- Shifting from a designated length of instruction to a length that better suits the learner's attention span and processing stamina

- Shifting the moment of learning from an arbitrary time and date to the moment of critical need

On the subject of time-shifted training, one of the most exciting emerging models is Just-in-Time Training. JITT is a framework for delivering the precise instruction needed and wanted at the time and place it's most needed and wanted. In the last chapter, we talked about the 16-year-old girl who learned to pick a lock at the exact moment she needed to get access. Boom! Mic drop. This is the sweet spot of training and learning. It's the moment in time where the training is most relevant and the interest level and engagement of the learner is at the apex. This is the moment when the horse you've been leading to the water, is ready and eager to drink.

Some of the most game-changing innovations are evolving around JITT training, and we'll explore in later chapters how Flipped Learning is a foundation, a framework, and a facilitator of Just-In-Time Training.

For now, we'll close with a powerful metaphor from FLGI Research Fellow Robert Talbert. Talbert sees Flipped Learning as an "operating system" and other instructional models as applications. What Windows, Mac OS, or Linux are to your computer, Flipped Learning is to your training program. Flipped Learning is the operating system on which applications like gamification, adaptive learning, social learning, micro learning, personalized learning, and just in time learning can run efficiently and effectively. Flipped Learning doesn't compete with these training concepts; it supports them. Flipped Learning is the foundation that makes high-quality training more possible, more responsive, and more relevant to more learners.

If we do our job well, when you put this book down you'll see why and how Flipped Learning is the ideal foundation, framework, and facilitator for your corporate training program—and you'll embrace it.

We press on!

Chapter 4

"Schooling" Vs. "Training"

It's time to tackle the big question at the center of this book. Are we talking apples and oranges or six in one hand and a half a dozen of the other?

In other words, to what extent is Flipped Learning in formal education and Flipped Learning in corporate training similar or different?

In this chapter, we compare "schooling" to "training." The goal? To determine to how much what we know about Flipped Learning in K-12 education applies to training in the business world.

Where Flipped Learning is concerned, perhaps there is no significant difference between schooling and training. But what if corporate training and talent development are so different from schooling that many of the core insights we've gleaned from academia don't apply? Simply said, what can corporate trainers learn from flippers in K-12 and higher education?

Let's jump in.

IN THE BEGINNING

We started with a hail of questions, synapses firing like a submachine gun's rat-tat-tat as one thought after another whizzed through our minds:

1. What is the fundamental rationale for business training?

2. What are the biggest pain points in business training?

3. What are some of the typical attitudes toward training among management and staff?

4. What is the typical business training schedule?

5. To what extent do training approaches vary between different business populations and business models?

6. How does turnover impact how training is considered, planned, and delivered?

7. To what extent are trainers accountable for results?

8. How is training efficacy determined?

9. What happens when learners aren't learning?

The questions became a starting point for our exploration. What eventually emerged included a core set of common issues between schooling and training, but we ultimately landed on a unique set of challenges that primarily impact training professionals.

We separated our findings into three categories:

- Where schooling and training are the same

- Where schooling and training are different

- Where the distinctions between schooling and training are murky and require more study.

Here's a practical example:

Video has become an increasingly popular tool in both schooling and corporate training. The debate has long been settled: video can be a very effective teaching tool in both learning scenarios. But here's where things get interesting. Some deep-pocketed companies are spending the cost of a Hollywood B movie to produce training videos. The aim? Create a professional training tool that will engage trainees and impress management.

Meanwhile, in the education space, the data show that amateur video created by the teacher is typically more engaging to students than slickly produced video created by professional production teams. Why? Relationships.

It turns out that the relationship with the teacher supersedes high production values when it comes to student engagement.

Hmm. To quote the great corporate trainer, Edgar Bergen, "Who'd a thunk it?"

FAcilitation

Do relationships matter in corporate training videos? If so, how many corporate training bucks have been flushed down the toilet on Spielberg-Lucas-Howard–level productions, when in-house talent and an iPhone video would have hit the target?

You can see evidence of this phenomenon all over YouTube. A company spends grand-theft dollars to produce a video that gets 200 views (mostly from friends and family).

Meanwhile, back at mom and dad's place, some tween in his bedroom bangs out a video in a few hours that goes viral to two million viewers. Are there any engagement lessons here for corporate trainers?

Now fast forward. On the leading edge of Flipped Learning in education, instructional videos are being made by students. Duhhh! Of course, who can better relate to a student than another student? Who would the typical student rather listen to—a cool peer or some over-the-hill 25-year-old teacher? We ask again, are there any engagement lessons here for corporate trainers?

THE BIG "PAIN POINTS" OF SCHOOLING AND TRAINING

After chasing our questions down one rabbit hole after another, we decided that looking at schooling and training through the lens of pain points was the most relevant. After all, if this book can't solve some of the biggest problems in corporate training, you might as well be watching past episodes of the White House Press briefings.

However, if you've been involved in schooling or training, you know that there are some common instructional issues that have stalked teachers and trainers since the beginning of time. Not surprisingly, the first is time.

PAIN POINT # 1—WHEN? THAT IS THE QUESTION

Schooling—Both schooling and training take time. Academia solved this problem with school bells, school semesters, and school years. Though there are pockets of raging resistance around whether school days should begin later or school years extended, mandating K-12 school time is almost universally accepted. The pain point for teachers is "how do I find the time to ensure that every student learns all they are expected to learn in the time allotted?" The phrase to underline here is "every student."

The traditional line-'em-up in rows and teach from the front of the room model was designed to "reach" every student. This Industrial Age–approach was about moving herds of students through a subject in a specific period of time. Despite the growing threat to this assembly-line teaching strategy, the "sage on the stage" model has "worked" for over 100 years.

But today the difference between "reaching" and actually "teaching" is more broadly understood. More importantly, the massive gap between "teaching" and "learning" is now on the radar screen of teachers and trainers, and is driving the global interest in new approaches—including Flipped Learning.

Training—On the business training side, time is a factor for different reasons. In schooling, learning is the primary objective of all stakeholders. In business training, learning takes a back seat to getting things done. Training is typically viewed by trainees (and managers) as "time away" from that thing you're being paid to do called work. Simply said, training is disconnected from work.

In a Bottom Line Performance survey, 150 L&D professionals were asked what challenges they face when attempting to deliver effective training. The results were published in their 2017 Learning and Remembering Report. Number one on the list was time. " . . . Organizations face time restrictions every day. This is especially true when trying to squeeze training into employees' busy schedules."[1]

In a March 2017 article published by ATD, Julie Winkle Giulioni echoes the point. She cites a survey of 300 L&D professionals which agreed that time is the biggest challenge:

"From nonexistent lead-times to laughable turnaround times to no time to offer the best they have to give, too few hours in the day and days in the month present a constant challenge. As a result, it's critical for learning professionals to develop strategies for managing the tyranny of time."[2]

Flipped Learning is fundamentally about time. Flipped Learning began with asking, "What is the best use of the instructor's time?" It evolved to ask, "What is the best use of the learner's time?

Indeed, "time shifting" is a core principal in Flipped Learning. In formal education, one of the primary results of Flipped Learning is more effective and efficient use of time by the instructor and the learner.

Today, the leading edge of Flipped Learning in corporate training is exploring ways to shift instruction to the best time for teaching and learning to occur.

In the coming pages, we'll explore in depth how Flipped Learning uses time shifting to address the vicious conflict between "time" and "class size." We'll also look at how Flipped Learning can be used to reconnect learning to work and move the focus from training to learning.

PAIN POINT # 2— PUHLEEZE DON'T BE BORING

Whether you're a teacher or a trainer, this is a really bad time to be boring. Many of your students and trainees come with preexisting conditions— they are "alive" and prefer to stay that way. This is why as far back as any of your trainees can remember one of their greatest fears was the threat of being bored to death.

Today this condition has a few new names, like ADD, and ADHD. Now hordes of millennials are showing up at school and work with the attention span of 140 characters or six seconds—whichever is shortest. If that's not enough to make you question your career choice, you are also competing with a never-ending stream of distractions vying for your learners' attention.

So whether you're a teacher or trainer, being boring is the first on the list of deadly sins to avoid. Indeed, the first rule of creating training that doesn't suck is, "don't be boring." Can you imagine how corporate training would change if all CLOs had this principle tattooed on their forehead?

Schooling—Teachers routinely struggle to vanquish boring and engage students. Most have experimented with a myriad of strategies to "hook" students. Of course, formal education and large parts of the curriculum are mandatory, so it's an uphill battle to engage all students on every subject. Even the most dynamic, captivating, and creative teacher will not be able to engage "every" student, every day, on every topic.

"A student who shows up on time for school and listens respectfully in class might appear fully engaged to outside observers, including teachers. But other measures of student engagement, including the student's emotional and cognitive involvement with the course material, may tell a different story," writes Ming-Te Wang, assistant professor of psychology in education in the School of Education and of psychology in the Kenneth P. Dietrich School of Arts and Sciences at the University of Pittsburgh.[3] In other words, students can appear engaged even while all tangible measures say otherwise. Though their lights are on, it doesn't guarantee anyone's home. How discouraging!

Training—Like teachers, corporate trainers often suffer through the indignity of speaking to a room of disengaged bodies. The trainees are in their seats, their eyes are open, but their minds have left the building. This is especially true in compliance training where the aim for both trainee and trainer is often to check the box.

Bryant Nielson, a corporate trainer and Managing Director for CapitalWave Inc., writes: "Probably the number one thing keeping corporate training programs from producing results is that employees aren't engaged. This can be the result of many different factors—learners might not find the information valuable or relevant, the training might be too advanced or too easy for the audience, or the seminar room simply might be too warm and the instructor's voice too soothing. For whatever reason . . . Traditional programs just aren't doing it for them."[4]

Flipped Learning can't turn a frog into a prince or make painfully boring subject matter riveting. But Flipped Learning can elevate engagement and reduce the torture of learning dull material in two ways:

First, Flipped Learning shifts direct instruction of dry material to bite-sized videos that students can easily consume. The subject matter may still be dreary and tiring, but the excruciating pain is limited to a more tolerable five-minute clip.

Secondly, traditional class time is now available for "active learning"—doing something with the material learned through the video. The focus shifts from the teacher lecturing to the learners creatively applying what they've learned, guided and assisted by the teacher. Now the class time is transformed into a dynamic, interactive learning environment.

Google "student engagement" and you'll drown in studies confirming that the overwhelming majority of students perceive themselves to be more engaged in a flipped classroom. Even drop-dead boring compliance material can be resurrected with activity. How can we make this claim so confidently? Because doing something, anything is simply more engaging than quietly sitting and passively listening.

The promise of Flipped Learning in corporate training is a very exciting new frontier that we've just begun to explore. On the leading edge of flipped corporate training, L&D professionals are now exploring how even lifeless compliance training can become less boring by shifting instruction to a time when it's most relevant.

Bob Mosher is the chief learning evangelist for APPLY Synergies. In March 2017 he wrote an intriguing article published in Chief Learning Officer titled "Compliance Training: Cheers or Jeers?" He writes insightfully about the do-it-because-we-have-to nature of compliance training that often makes the process boring and dreaded.

Mosher argues that "for the most part, we've created an event-based solution for a workflow/performance problem." He doesn't dismiss the need for a basic introduction to compliance issues, but perhaps his most powerful insight is that "performing in a compliant way happens in the workflow; that's where our solutions need to target."[5] Aha!

Later in this chapter, we'll explain why Flipped Learning is an essential piece of the solution Mosher is suggesting.

PAIN POINT # 3—DID THEY LEARN ANYTHING? HOW DO WE KNOW?

These are the two questions teachers, principals, superintendents, education policy makers, and, increasingly, corporate trainers and their CEOs are asking.

Schooling—Accountability for teaching and learning is a top priority in the formal education universe. The National Assessment of Educational Progress (NAEP) and The Programme for International Student Assessment (PISA) have become valued and feared report cards on the efficacy of formal education. PISA and NAEP press stories broadcasting how well educators and students are doing have turned up the heat on all stakeholders. Today, impatience with instructional models that fail to deliver results has reached a high-water mark.

The search for what works leads many teachers and schools to Flipped Learning. In 2014, 38% of teachers had flipped a lesson. But do students learn more through Flipped Learning? How do we know?

We went on a treasure hunt to find evidence of how successful Flipped Learning is in promoting student learning and found that we weren't the first to embark on that journey. One list we discovered, put together by some teachers in the Jackson Local Schools in Massillon, Ohio, provided a veritable treasure chest of articles that all spoke to the efficacy of a flipped approach to learning.[6] We dug a little deeper and found the following excerpts compelling.

The Tulsa World reported on the success Spartan College of Aeronautics and Technology has had in flipping their pilot training programs:

"The Federal Aviation Administration requires Spartan and other aeronautics schools to maintain an 80 percent first-time combined pass rate for the two tests aspiring pilots must take, the hands-on FAA flight test and the written FAA knowledge test.

The combined first-time pass rate under the old, traditional learning style program was 83.9 percent. . . . The combined first-time pass rate for the new [Flipped Learning] program is 96 percent, a more than 12 percentage point increase."[7]

Combine the increased test scores with both the cost and time savings of students avoiding retraining due to failure, and that's an amazing success for both the students and the school!

Another article, this one from U.S. News & World Report, addressed the way Flipped Learning specifically applied to STEM (science, technology, engineering, and math) classes:

"At Villanova, [Randy] Weinstein [associate dean for academic affairs for Villanova's College of Engineering] helped lead a pilot program for flipping engineering courses. New data from the program given to U.S. News shows the bottom third of students' grades were more than 10 percent higher than in a traditional classroom (the difference between a D+ and a C) and more than 3 percent higher for the class as a whole (moving from a C+ to a B-).

"Scott Freeman, a principal lecturer at the University of Washington, flipped his introductory biology class to help improve a 17 percent failure rate. . . In the end, the course's failure rate dropped to about 4 percent, and the number of students earning A's increased to about 24 percent from 14 percent."[8]

Still need convincing? EmergingEdTech reported that the College of Westchester in White Plains, New York, piloted a Flipped Learning program on a very limited scope, and yet still saw positive results pointing toward success. The pilot was approached as a scientific experiment:

"Both quantitative and qualitative results from the partial flipped classed pilot have been very encouraging. Average grades increased, and even better, DFW [D/F/Withdrawing] rates significantly decreased. From a qualitative perspective, 94% of students responded that they liked this approach to learning and 72% indicated that this approach 'Helped [them] learn the material better.'[9]

Here, not only did the test results show improved scores, but the students themselves responded positively to the new approach—and as we will continue to explore, student engagement is a huge part of the battle.

Another scientific approach to the success of a Flipped Learning model, reported by The Economist, was taken by Louis Deslauriers in his physics course for engineering students at the University of British Columbia. His approach:

"The students were split into groups at the start of their course, and for the first 11 weeks, all went to traditionally run lectures given by well-regarded and experienced teachers. In the 12th week, one of the groups was switched to a style of teaching known as deliberate practice, which inverts the traditional university model.

"At the end of the test week, Dr. Deslauriers surveyed the students and gave them a voluntary test (sold as useful exam practice, and marked on a 12-point scale) to see how much they had learned in that week and what they thought of the new teaching method. The results were striking . . . The traditionally taught group's average score was 41%, compared with 74% for the experimental group—even though the experimental group did not manage to cover all the material, it was supposed to, whereas the traditional group did."[10]

Did you catch that? Even covering less material, the experimental group learned and retained more than the traditionally taught group.

We could pull countless other stories of success, but we hope the evidence here has been enough to establish that Flipped Learning is clearly moving the needle in education.

Training—Measuring the impact of training has percolated to the top of the agenda in L&D circles as well. Assessment issues in corporate training are as complex, murky, and debated as in formal education. Many new models, tools, and strategies have been developed since Donald

Kirkpatrick's four levels of evaluation in the 1950s. Yet it's still debatable whether most corporate trainers or CEOs can tell whether their training dollars are leading to meaningful learning.

"Measuring impact seems basic, but most companies simply don't do it. McKinsey research finds that only 50 percent of organizations even bother to keep track of participants' feedback about training programs. Worse, only 30 percent use any other kind of metric," writes Aaron DeSmet, Monica McGurk, and Elizabeth Schwartz in the McKinsey Quarterly.[11]

Ask experts how much learning is transferred from training to the workplace, and you'll fall into a Grand Canyon–sized gap. On one bank there's the mythical 10% from David L. Georgenson;[12] on the other, the more substantiated 62% from researchers Alan M. Saks and Monica Belcourt.[13]

Indeed, as late as 2010, only one-quarter of the 1,440 respondents to a McKinsey survey said their training programs measurably improved business performance. Apparently, there was little notable progress when the survey was updated in 2014.[14]

From a 30,000-foot view, it appears that corporate training on planet Earth is largely a gargantuan leap of faith.

Flipped Learning is too new to corporate training to have the headline-grabbing track record it has in schooling. This is clearly an area where more research, evidence, and work are needed.

But here is what we do know:

The Brandon Hall Group's 2016 Training Benchmarking Study offered some relevant insights that speak to the efficacy of Flipped Learning in corporate training. Among the key findings:

- The classroom is still king in terms of use—it's chosen 22 percent more than any other modality. It's the second most effective modality. Coaching/mentoring is seen as more effective for the third consecutive year, while usage is 37 percent less.

- E-learning is the most expensive learning experience to develop, and video learning is the least expensive. But e-learning is utilized 28 percent more often.[15]

David Wentworth, Principle Learning Analyst at the Brandon Hall Group, notes that "Technology has provided learning with more delivery options than ever before. Social media tools, mobile devices, HD video, and more have dramatically expanded the breadth and depth of the learning ecosystem. However, at the center of all this remains the classroom. And the instructor-led classroom is still the predominant way learning is delivered—by a wide margin."[16]

If you are interested in Flipped Learning in corporate training, these bits of data should make you smile. In summary:

- Coaching and mentoring were found to be the most effective training modality.

- Face-to-face instructor-led classrooms are the second most effective and most-used training modality

- Video learning is the least expensive

Experiential

61

Any practitioner trained in Flipped Learning will immediately recognize the elements of Flipped Learning in this data.

And there's more …

The third most effective modality in the benchmarking study is on-the-job training. Drawing from the McKinsey study cited earlier, McKinsey analysts Liz Gryger, Tom Saar, and Patti Schaar wrote:

"As companies try to replicate or scale up their training across more geographies, alternative ways of delivering it will become necessary. In addition, our experience shows that on-the-job training is most effective when it is reinforced through some sort of formal teaching and feedback loop."[17]

If we connect the dots, we begin to see the outline of what's included in the most effective and optimal training mix: coaching, mentoring, face-to-face instruction, and video. Hmm . . . this is beginning to look a lot like Flipped Learning.

What else do we know that might be relevant?

In the benchmarking study, the fourth most effective modality was informal peer-to-peer learning and high on the list was in-person games and simulations. But here's the big takeaway: *of the eight most effective modalities in this study, seven are features of Flipped Learning or modalities that Flipped Learning enhances. Boom! Mic drop.*

The bottom line? Flipped Learning combines the most used, least expensive, and most effective training modalities in corporate training.

The Road Ahead

The emerging picture shows promise and possibilities for Flipped Learning in corporate training, but the truth is we're just scratching the surface. We're going to connect more dots a bit later that will elevate this discussion even further.

For now, we'll close this section with a comment from David Grebow. Grebow is the CEO of KnowledgeStar, a corporate learning thought leader and author of an upcoming book published by ATD called *Minds at Work*.

Grebow has a long and fascinating career in corporate learning. When IBM started to question whether their staff was learning anything from the $500 million dollars they were spending on e-learning, they formed IBM Institute for Advanced Learning and asked Grebow to be the co-director.

He observed that "programs which looked great were also great at disabling the learning process. Programs that at first glance looked dumb were excellent at enabling the learning process and really getting results. Learning how to see the difference started me on the path toward where I am today."[18]

Grebow wrote about Flipped Learning in 2013 when he first started working on flipping a corporate class:

"Now to the Big Question: I cannot understand WHY in K-12 grades and colleges and universities classes are being flipped every week, and I have yet to hear about it happening in a corporate, educational environment . . .

A flipped class in a corporation makes even more sense since everyone is under greater time constraints and learning has become more and more performance based—what you know how to do versus what you know. So being able to practice with others and with an 'expert' either in the room or on the screen would be a perfect fit…

We've been working on flipping a corporate class lately and looked for other examples. We came up empty handed. If anyone has heard of a company smart enough to use the flipped class model, please let us know."[19]

In 2013 Grebow couldn't find companies flipping corporate training. Today the model is gaining traction in corporate training circles around the world. The writing on the wall suggests that we are entering the golden age of Flipped Learning in corporate training.

PAIN POINT #4 RESISTANCE TO CHANGE

K-12 education has been in a tumultuous state of reform for over 100 years. Historically, reforms have taken different forms because the motivations of reformers have differed.

Which brings us to two of the elements that schooling and training have in common:

- Both schooling and training involve an ongoing battle between those who are leaning into the future and those who want to continue doing instruction the way they've always done it.

- Both schooling and training involve mastering a set of the mixed martial arts–caliber skills required to manage different stakeholders with different agendas and priorities.

Schooling—The drivers behind resistance to change in formal education are the subjects of entire books. The list includes the neuroscience of survival, tradition, ego, culture, fear of failure, job security, competing agendas, "not invented here," and "because I just don't want to." Adding to the melee is a diverse list of stakeholders that have to "buy in" to change any educational system. Those stakeholders include parents, politicians, federal boards, state boards, school boards, unions, principals, teachers, and, yes, students. Each group has the power to derail any change to the way learning happens.

Perhaps, the big takeaway from the history of K-12 education reform is that change is hard, but it's possible— and it's worth it.

Training—When we look at resistance to change in the corporate training world, the players are wearing different uniforms, but many of the same dynamics are on the field: human nature, tradition, ego, culture, competing agendas, yada, yada, blah, blah, blah.

The stakeholder roster includes the CLO, HR, the CEO, CFO, division managers, trainers and, yes, trainees who "just don't want to." As in schooling, any of these players in the training ecosystem can toss a monkey wrench into the process of changing the way learning happens.

Sharing insights from the 2017 Bottom-Line Performance Learning and Remembering Survey of 150 L&D professionals, Holly Hilton wrote:

> "Lots of respondents also mentioned their struggle to get managers and stakeholders to buy into a new training program. For example, maybe everyone agrees your company training is outdated and deserves a fresh new look. But one stakeholder isn't convinced that

training is the answer to your problem. They argue that past training experiences failed and wonder, "What will training really fix?"[20]

Again, the big takeaway from reviewing the evolving history of corporate training is that change is hard, but it's possible, and it's worth it.

Flipped Learning—We've gleaned some valuable insights about dealing with resistance to change from the experiences of introducing Flipped Learning around the globe. Many are transferable to corporate training. Here are just a few:

1. Change takes time. Changing a learning system and culture is a marathon, not a sprint. Understanding this from the word go will help you to temper your expectations and pace yourself as needed.

2. Change is a process. Moving to a Flipped Learning model requires coordinating resources, people, time, tools, technology, tactics and strategy. Most importantly, it requires clear, consistent, and constant communication between all stakeholders.

3. Start with the people who get it. We've seen three kinds of "change agents": lone rangers, enthusiastic optimists, and pragmatists who know how to find and engage early supporters. Guess which one is most likely to succeed.

4. We've seen how change can be driven from four directions:

    a. Bottom up: When the learners and instructors embrace change, a powerful movement can start that drives change across the organization.

b. Top down: Change that starts at the top is often notoriously resisted. But even grassroots movements need top-down support to scale to potential.

c. Local conditions: The needs of a local group can drive change that ignores what the rest of an organization or the world is doing.

d. Global forces: Competition from the division down the hall, the company across town, or a start-up on the other side of the globe can drive changes at the local level.

Figure 4.1 The Four Forces Driving Flipped Adoption

Flipped Learning started at the grassroots level, eventually gained top-down support, and then became a global movement localized for specific countries, cultures, and settings. Where might your change process begin?

Finding the Critical Balance

One of the biggest lessons we've learned from our research, interviews and our consulting practice is that good intentions are insufficient to successfully drive the change to Flipped Learning in a corporate training setting.

Effective execution requires a balanced alignment of business strategy with training tactics.

Business Strategy   **Training Tactics**

Aligned and Balanced

Figure 4.2 Aligning Business Strategy and Training

Further, aligning training with strategy requires a keen business-specific understanding of the internal and external forces in play.

Dave Ulrich, Rensis Likert Professor of Business at the University of Michigan, writes that an "outside in" perspective is critical. This strategic view includes the social, technological, economic, political, environmental, and demographic concerns of inside and outside stakeholders. This means employees and managers as well as investors, suppliers, partners, dealers, distributors, customers and the community.[21]

Internal   External

Stakeholders

Figure 4.3 Balancing the Strategic Interests of Internal and External Stakeholders

Historically, this kind if holistic strategic thinking has been beyond the scope and skillset of L&D professionals. Writing in Training Magazine, Ross Tartell, Ph.D., Adjunct Associate Professor, Psychology, Columbia University notes that, "We know we must tie training to organizational strategy and business needs. Why can't we figure out how to do it?

I think our dilemma is a result of the 'Knowing vs. Doing' gap. Most of the profession intellectually knows what to do—the problem is turning an intellectual understanding into action."[22]

This point was recently underscored by one of our international clients. Their team of highly skilled learning and development professionals had been working to revamp their multimillion-dollar training program through Flipped Learning. They reported to us:

"We have been working and defining our strategy for the last four plus years and we are well on the journey with great management support which is flowing down through markets and countries. We also have full marketing support/ sales and market research knowledge."

Despite, this rosy report, they were seeking our help because the buy-in from their trainees was around 40 percent. They were convinced that their strategy was sound and their problems were tactical.

To effectively drive change, we've found that it requires a granular, on the ground, tactical understanding. But it also takes a big picture, 30,000-foot, strategic perspective to see how all of the relevant dots connect. In short, tactics **and** strategy.

How critical is this point? Perhaps the significance is best summed up by words often attributed the Chinese general and philosopher Sun Tzu. On the relationship between strategy and tactics he states:

"Strategy without tactics is the slowest route to victory. Tactics without strategy is the noise before defeat."

Pushing Back on Resistance to Change

We'll close with one of our favorite "overcoming resistance to change" stories.

For decades, Los Angles was known for its car culture, its vast, expansive freeways, and an embarrassingly impotent public transportation system. Smog, skyrocketing gas prices, and traffic gridlock finally drove city managers to develop a mass transit plan. In 1976 preliminary work began, and a decade later, construction started. The Blue Line finally opened on July 14, 1990.

Observing the way many Angelinos were persuaded to make the leap from a car culture to one that embraces mass transit offers some tips for introducing Flipped Learning in the corporate training space.

At first, it was common to see trains coming and going with barely a soul on board. Some trains on the system had just two cars, and even they were largely empty. Those of us who lived in the city would watch smugly from our cars as the empty trains went by. Who would ever leave the convenience and comfort of their vehicles to wait on trains and share transportation with strangers? As months went by, the expensive transit program began to look like a big mistake—a glaring boondoggle on display for all the world to see. Yet, despite appearances, the trains kept coming and going as planned, whether there were ten passengers on board or none.

Today Los Angeles has multiple lines, with multiple train cars running daily. All are routinely filled with passengers. Though LA will likely never rival the who-needs-a-car culture of New York City, through planning, consistent execution, and persistence, Los Angeles made unimaginable change happen.

Whether we're talking mass transit, schooling, or corporate training, driving change is hard, but it's possible—and it's worth it!

PAIN POINT # 5—DID THE LEARNING STICK?

Perhaps the area where schooling and training differ most is in the area of learning loss.

Schooling—Generally speaking, teachers operate in air-tight compartments called school years.

Historically, they were responsible for getting students to the year-end test with good grades. When the year was finished, off the students went. Though learning loss has long been a concern in formal education, the culture of schooling makes passing the tests and moving from grade level to grade level more important to students and some teachers.

Today, cultivating students' ability to apply what they've learned is the new frontier in K-12 education. But in the corporate training space, it's always been the tacit expectation that employees going through a training event would come back ready to apply what they've learned.

Time to dance with the elephant in the room.

Training—Billions of training dollars are spent every year by companies large and small. Yet the "forgetting curve" is astounding. How much corporate training is ultimately forgotten? Some researchers cite numbers so high only your dog can hear them. If you're reading this book, you've likely seen loss estimates as high as 90 percent at just seven days after training. If these numbers are valid, the image of trainers filling the trainees' heads with knowledge is largely false. The appropriate image is more like knowledge going in one ear and blowing out the other in a surprisingly short period of time.

Volumes have been written about this problem, so we're not going to waste a lot of ink on this. If you're new to the problem, simply google Hermann Ebbinghaus and brew a big pot of coffee.

Suffice it to say that given the dollars, time, and resources involved, it's reasonable to argue that learning loss may be the biggest problem in corporate training. Indeed, it is possible that the reason learning loss doesn't top everyone's list of the challenges L&D professionals face is that many have simply come to accept and ignore this massive elephant in the room.

But enough of the problems and pain points, let's make a mad dash to exploring solutions.

EVOLVING MINDS

Remember your times tables? If you're of a certain age, you probably do. "Drill and kill," they called it; and when asked to recite those multiplication tables, you had to be ready to stand and deliver. Keeping those numbers in our heads is still useful, but the truth is, memorizing times tables is no longer necessary. Virtually all of us have calculators in our pockets. If you don't know your times tables, so what? No one will die. You can quickly and easily get the answer when you need it.

A rapidly growing school of thinkers are awakening to how this ubiquitous tool in our pockets can radically impact instruction, teaching, learning, and learning loss. Since we can access nearly unlimited information on our phones, the game has changed—and so have the questions raised.

This new school is exploring questions like:

- What happens if we shift the focus of training from remembering information to applying information?

- What happens if we shift the location of training to the place where that information is needed, wanted, relevant, and in context?

- What happens if we forget about learning loss, and focus instead on rapid learning aggregation and accessibility?

- What if we support this new approach with the necessary training and support systems to make this model viable?

This school of thought is playing out in emerging trends like Microlearning, mobile learning, social learning, and a wholesale rethinking of on-the-job training. Many of the pioneers of these trends believe that we are exploring the most exciting and promising frontier in corporate training. Part of the enthusiasm is based on the fact that the tools exist, the platforms exist, the global infrastructure exists, the instructional models exist, and the know-how exists to solve training problems that have existed since the beginning of time!

All that's needed is a blueprint for making all of these apparently disparate trends, concepts, ideas, models, platforms, strategies, techniques, and tools play nicely together.

BREAKING NEWS: That blueprint also exists, and it's called Flipped Learning 3.0. In the coming sections, we'll explain why all of the new trends, tools, models, and platforms are "apps" in search of an operating system. We'll also explain why Flipped Learning is the operating system that enables and supports them all.

Now I pass the keyboard back to Jon, who will get really practical. He will explain the best practices in Flipped Learning (Chapter 5), how to design lessons for the Individual Space (Chapter 6), and how to design lessons in the Group Space (Chapter 7).

Chapter 5

Best Practices of Flipped Learning

Ashley Walton is a senior training consultant at Traveler's Insurance. She and her team are responsible for onboarding new employees in their commercial insurance writing division. Before 2008 new trainees flew to their headquarters in Hartford, Connecticut, for a two-week training. The training consisted mostly of sit-and-get activities and was somewhat effective for that time. However, when the recession of 2008 hit, they realized they needed a better way. They needed a method that cost less and which produced better results. Over the course of the decade since, they have brought in elements of online learning, blended learning, and now Flipped Learning. Though she says they still have more steps to go, she sees Flipped Learning as foundational to their continued training programs.

As we did research for this book, we sought out corporate trainers who had utilized Flipped Learning in their practice.

We interviewed dozens of people and heard their stories. They discussed why they got started with Flipped Learning, what they did right, and what they did wrong. Occasionally we cringed as they shared some aspect of their training. They had committed some of the "cardinal sins" of what not to do when flipping the learning. Some had realized this and adapted, and some continued using practices we knew were not going to work. I have been helping organizations implement Flipped Learning for over a decade, and have found some best practices which need to be a part of any successful Flipped Learning program. These best practices come from both research and real-world implementations. In this chapter, we will explore a few of the key questions and lay out best practices.

WHAT IF THEY DON'T DO THE PRE-WORK?

The most common question asked about Flipped Training is this: what if the learner does not do the pre-work? (Henceforth I will also refer to the pre-work as Individual Space learning). Flipped Learning sounds great in a tenth-grade math class where students are expected to do homework, but trainers can't typically send employees home with homework! As mentioned earlier, herein lies one of the fundamental differences between the education sector and corporate training. Employees are not in a class for one hour a day for a year with their "teacher." Trainees have real jobs, and most likely, training is designed to improve job performance, teach critical new skills, develop soft skills, or prepare them to do a specific task. Training should advance the mission of the organization or enhance its profitability. So how do you structure your training such that trainees come prepared for the Group Space?

Since you usually can't expect employees to do "homework," the training must be structured such that time is built into the training for the pre-work. This method has become known as the In-Flip, or, rather, the In-class Flip. In this model, there is no expectation that people will come to the training with the work done; instead, time is provided in a variety of fashions for the pre-work to get done. For some companies, the trainees come to the class and trainees individually do the pre-work at the training center before the Group Space time. Others give employees fewer responsibilities so that they can get the pre-work done during work hours such that their face-to-face training time is maximized.

I chatted with a trainer at a call center for a major computer manufacturer, and he requires his call center employees to use some of the slow time to watch micro-videos on new products and implementations during the employees' typical work week. Then when the Group Space time is scheduled, the participants are ready to take a deeper dive.

Crystal Fernandes-Harris and Carrie Kirby, who lead training at the Day Pitney law firm in New York City, have had great success training legal staff. They expect the legal staff to complete the pre-work during the work day; however, they realize that the assistants have busy jobs and expecting them to get pre-work done is a big ask. Thus, they approached the lawyers who oversaw the assistants and convinced them that the training was valuable and would, in the long run, make the assistants' jobs more effective and efficient. Since the lawyers saw the value in training they made allowances for the pre-work. Some of the trainees had to ask for additional time, which they were given but overall, getting the pre-work done has not proved to be a major problem. The training has been a great success, and they attribute the success to the buy-in from the lawyers and the improvements the training has accomplished.

Another way to get learners do the pre-work is to expect that they do it on their own time. This may not work in many contexts, but it will in some. Take, for example, Cathy Mongeau, a Digital Learning Design Manager at AbbVie Pharmaceutical who is responsible for training AbbVie's sales representatives for a few of their products. She expects her salespeople to do the work on their own time. Salespeople are incentivized to learn because for them to sell a specific drug, they must pass a certification exam and are paid on a commission basis. As exempt employees, this model works. For non-exempt employees, expecting them to do pre-work on their own time should not be required.

Patty Evans, Manager of e-Learning and Training at Yardi, a company that supports rental properties around the world, convinces middle managers to require the pre-work from new hires. Before a new group starts, she sends emails to all managers—and copies their bosses—to encourage the pre-work. Since all new employees must pass tests before they work with clients, there is an incentive to engage with the work. The training typically lasts four weeks, and during the face-to-face time (some of which takes place virtually), the importance of the pre-work is explained to the trainees. They even go so far as to include answers to the certification exam questions only in the pre-work. Evans has found that these solutions solve many of the issues of a lack of engagement in the pre-work.

Another example of a trainer who expects people to do the work on their own time is Freddie Batista, a fireman, EMT, e-learning coach, and learning entrepreneur. His first passion was firefighting, but soon realized he had a knack for training and specifically e-learning. He has run many continuing education classes with firemen, and he expects those coming to his face-to-face classes to have done the pre-work. The technology tool he uses tracks those who did not complete the pre-work. Thus, if you don't do the pre-work, you can't come to class. He has found this effective, and his programs have had great success.

Taking all of these cases together reveals a continuum. You can either provide the pre-work time during the class, figure out how to provide time in some other creative means, or expect employees to do the work on their own time. The image below should help. Ultimately, you'll need to decide where your training fits on this continuum. A lot depends on your corporate culture, how busy your people are, and what value your organization places on the specific learning outcomes.

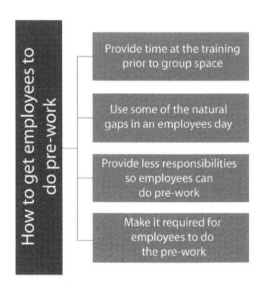

Figure 5.1: How to get trainees to do the pre-work

ACCOUNTABILITY

In many ways, the flipped class model succeeds or fails based on the degree to which learners interact with the Individual Space work. If they don't read the article or don't watch the video, then the training is doomed to fail. To that end, learners must be held accountable for completing the work. There are a variety of tracking tools which monitor the percentage of engagement in digital content. These tools measure things such as whether they watched a video, at what speed they watched the video, and what percentage of the video they watched, and many now allow for questions to be added either in the middle or at the end of a video. There are also tools that work similarly with reading. These tools track how many minutes a learner is in a text, and lesson designers can intersperse questions throughout. When learners know that instructors are checking pre-work, our experience is that they will acquiesce and get it done.

We don't want to browbeat learners into completing the pre-work, but sometimes they need to be held accountable. Our experience is that the best way to ensure that learners interact in the Individual Space is to make the Group Space indispensable and valuable. Adult learners need to see the practical nature of the training, and when these needs are addressed, they will buy in and embrace Flipped Learning.

WHO CREATES THE CONTENT?

In most instances, Flipped Learning is associated with videos watched before the Group Space time, and the question is often asked: who creates the content? I see four options:

- Create your own content

- Use content online from free sites like YouTube

- Use content online by training platforms like Udemy

- Outsource content creator to custom design professional products for in-house use

A continuum can represent this create-curate-outsource debate.

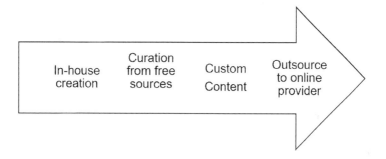

Figure 5.2: Who Creates the Flipped Content?

On one side is trainer creation and on the other is outsourcing for custom content. Which you choose depends on many factors including budget, the purpose of the training, time, and technical skills. At the Day Pitney law firm, Crystal Fernandes-Harris and Carrie Kirby, whom we met earlier, make a few of their videos in-house. They are primarily teaching software tools and find a simple screencast to be sufficient for their needs. Most of their training is also done with vendor-created videos, yet when they surveyed their learners, 78% preferred videos created by a "familiar voice."

Cathy Mongeau from AbbVie, whom we also met earlier, has a small green-screen studio where her team makes quick videos for their courses. However, for some projects, she has brought in professional video companies to produce the work for the Individual Space. Sue Czeropski, the lead trainer from Valin, a process control company, has used content from Udemy (an online course repository) as a precursor for engaging onsite training.

Each of these instructional designers took a different path, as did many of the trainers we interviewed. But we were interested to discover that most of them found that trainer-created videos were very effective. Some had used both vendors and in-house training, and they all felt that even though some of their videos were of a lower production value than vendor-provided videos, the overall courses were more effective when they used their own videos. It is, therefore, our recommendation that the trainers responsible for the group space should be the primary creators of the content. We've found that teaching is fundamentally about human interactions, and when the trainer delivers the individual space content, this brings credibility, builds relationships, and enhances learning. That said, there certainly are instances where using outside vendors makes sense. Ultimately, which method you choose depends on budget, time, and the degree to which the training adds value to your company.

SIMPLE COURSE DESIGN

Most of the Individual Space work is presented in an e-learning platform. Though most e-learning platforms are generally good, it is easy to for a course designer to make the course overly complex and convoluted. Designers should adhere to the rule that less is more and "simple" is best. This is where the art of teaching is pivotal because taking a complex idea or process and breaking it down into simple, manageable steps is hard. But when done well, this is where course participants will find the greatest success. Take time to think about the content of the course deeply and then do the extra work to make the design of the course intuitive. The fewer clicks, the better.

MAKING THE GROUP SPACE ESSENTIAL AND ENGAGING

We have seen first-time flippers make the mistake of re-teaching material during the Group Space time. This is one of the cardinal sins of Flipped Learning. Never, never, never re-teach what was presented in the Individual Space time. If you do this, you are telling every trainee who completed the pre-work that they didn't have to and everyone who did not complete the work that it was not necessary.

Bill McGrath, who trains emergency medical technicians, confessed to us that he re-lectured for those students who had not engaged with the flipped video. He quickly realized what a huge mistake that was and how he had to go back and make major changes to convince his students that the flipped videos were essential. Ashley Walton of Travelers Insurance also confessed to making this mistake. She told us that when they were in the Group Space the trainers would do the same things that were in the flipped videos. When she re-lectured, fewer trainees completed the pre-work, and the ones that did the pre-work complained how boring the presentations were because they had already learned it. To repeat: Never, never, never repeat what is in the flipped portion of the course in the Group Space.

This is not to say that you don't help trainees who did complete the pre-work and still struggle. But there must be an expectation that participants have done the pre-work before you will repeat material covered in the Individual Space.

MICROLEARNING

Though it is important to think about longer-term classes which might last a week or more, there are certainly other needs within a corporation for ongoing training. Employees have important jobs and are often too busy with their regular tasks to take time to go off-site for a day of training, let alone a week. Yet there is a constant need for people to update their skills, keep current on new trends, and see what is next. Microlearning can be a part of that solution. There are many articles and books discussing Microlearning, so we won't go into too much detail here.

Suffice it to say, Microlearning could be considered a component of Flipped Learning. If an employee needs to learn how to operate a specific function in a piece of accounting software, instead of going to the manual or attending an all-day training, they would be better served by an easily accessed repository of flipped videos. Most likely, a two-minute video will get them the answers they need and get them back to their job function. If a company decides to create or acquire these resources, then it is imperative that they are easy to access, well organized, and searchable.

But Microlearning does not just apply to software; it can also work with other skills. Call-center trainers, EMT trainers, and legal trainers all have used this model to help their employees function better on the job.

INTRODUCE CHOICE INTO THE TRAINING

Adults thrive when they have greater control of the learning. One way to give learners more control is to allow them to choose their own learning path. Some learners learn better via a flipped video, while others do better with text, and still others learn best via a hands-on activity. We found that the ideal Flipped Training model gives learners choices in both the way they learn and also the way they are assessed. Adopting choice boards gives more control to the learning to trainees. Below is a choice board which encompasses both the Individual and the Group Space. Note how it mirrors Bloom's Taxonomy. Each trainee must complete one activity from each column.

	Knowledge Understanding (Do in the Individual Space)	Application Level Activities (Do in the Group Space)	Higher Order Activities (Do in the Group Space)
Activity 1	Read document and take notes	Online Simulation	Role-playing activity
Activity 2	Watch flipped video and answer questions	Complete a series of application questions	Case-study activity

One mistake some trainers make is to provide too many choices. We do not recommend having an excessive number of choices as this can confuse the learner. Two or three options is usually sufficient. Clearly, it is more work to utilize multiple learning modalities, but it is important to realize that trainees come with different learning styles, preferences, and backgrounds. Accommodating for different learning styles can greatly enhance retention, which makes choice a valuable addition to any Flipped Training program.

DESIGN THE TRAINING WITH THE RIGHT PEOPLE

One of the biggest challenges to introducing Flipped Learning into an organization is having the right skill sets on the training team. Many trainers come from a traditional training paradigm, and some may come with little in the way of technical skills. To successfully implement Flipped Learning, there is a need for a variety of skills. Ideally, courses are designed by a team comprised of a project manager, a content expert, an instructional designer, somebody deeply immersed in e-learning software development, and face-to-face trainers who understand their role as facilitators instead of disseminators of knowledge.

Many of you reading this book might be saying, "I have to fill all those roles." If your team has limited personnel capital to pull off an involved training, the beauty of Flipped Training is that it can also be done on a shoestring budget. What is most important is to have the trainers understand that they should not use class time to disseminate knowledge, but rather to flip it on its head.

GOOD TEACHING ALWAYS COMES BACK TO RELATIONSHIPS

In my twenty-four years as a middle- and high-school science teacher, I realized that if I didn't build into the lives of my students, then the best-crafted lesson or the most active classroom activity would fall flat. People are built to be relational beings who need more than a cold training. I realize that the K-12 classroom is different than the corporate culture, but the fundamental truth is that when people feel connected with other humans, the benefits go beyond the learning and extend to an entire organization.

When I was the director of technology at the Joseph Sears School in Illinois, I led a lot of staff training. The best thing I did upon arrival at the school was to schedule a time with each of the staff members when I could get to know them and learn their strengths, their frustrations, and what they thought would take them to the next level. Those meetings paid dividends for the remainder of my time because I took the time to listen. When I later asked them to try something new, they were much more open to change.

Stephen Leib, a senior technical writer and planner at the Arizona Department of Health Services, summarized the factors that motivate adult learners. The first motivator was, "Social Relationships: to make new friends, to meet new associations and friendships."[1] Other studies have shown the positive correlation between positive human connections and learner outcomes.

We realize that not all training allows for deeper interaction and personal connection. But, to the degree that an organization can humanize the training, they should incorporate it into training. We also realize that incorporating relationship-building into a course may seem to decrease the ROI on the course.

Building relationships into training may seem daunting, but, in reality, successful programs rely on simple human interactions. In an article for the Association for Psychology Science, William Buskist gives the following tips to building rapport with adult learners:

- Learn to call your trainees by name when possible.

- Create and use personally relevant class examples.

- Arrive to class early and stay late—and chat with your trainees.

- Get online: use e-mail to increase accessibility to your trainees.

- Interact more, lecture less—emphasize active learning.

- Reward student comments and questions with verbal praise.

- Be enthusiastic about teaching and passionate about your subject matter.

- Lighten up—crack a joke now and then.

- Be humble and, when appropriate, self-deprecating.

- Make eye contact with each trainee—without staring, glaring, or flaring.

- When possible, learn something about your trainees' interests, hobbies, and aspirations.

- Be respectful.

- Don't forget to smile![2]

It seems simple—and it is—sort of. It takes extra energy and time to connect, but when you do, the effect of your training will increase.

NEXT

As we look further into flipping the corporate learning environment, we want to look at how to reimagine both the Individual Space and the Group Space.

Chapter 6

Designing Flipped Learning in the Individual Space

Designing a well-crafted flipped lesson requires a mental paradigm shift, an ability to build quality e-learning objects (videos, text-based, simulations, games, etc.), some creativity for face-to-face interactions, and a commitment to humanizing the training as much as possible. The next two chapters will focus on how to design training courses with Flipped Learning in mind. This chapter will focus on how to design lessons in the Individual Space, and the next will focus on how to design lessons in the Group Space. Recall that the Individual Space refers to the pre-learning activities which will be done before the face-to-face (or virtual face-to-face) interactions. The Group Space is the time when the trainer and the trainees are in the same location, whether that is in a physical or a virtual room.

BIG-PICTURE PLANNING

Though this chapter focuses on the Individual Space, it is important to look at the big picture first. We have all sat in classes or meetings where it was clear the course was not well planned, and therefore it lacked coherence. People have a hard time following a disorganized course. A well-designed course requires structure and planning. Below are a few quick suggestions to begin designing a flipped course:

- Ask: What is the purpose of this course?

- Determine a list of discrete objectives for the course. These objectives will form a list of training modules.

- Determine which parts of the training should occur during the Individual Space time.

- Determine which parts of the training should occur during the Group Space.

- Create learning objects (typically flipped videos or other e-learning objects) for the Individual Space.

- Design interactive and engaging activities for the Group Space.

Below is an example from Crystal Fernandes-Harris and Carrie Kirby from the Day Pitney law firm. They developed this outline for their course on how to use specific aspects of Microsoft Word in their firm.

Figure 6.1 Sample Outline

Due Date:		Session Dates:	
Main Topic	**Subtopic(s)**	**Technical Skills/ Knowledge**	**eLearning Content (All subtopics)**
Word TOC	TOC: Styles from Heading	Apply Word Heading Styles Customize Styles Generate automatic TOC Update TOC	**Tutorials** Word 2010 – Video 1 Word 2010 – Video 2 Word 2010 – Video 3
	TOC: Marked Headings	Mark headings to include in TOC Generate TOC manually Update TOC	**Quizzes** Word 2010 – Quiz 1 Word 2010 – Quiz 2 Word 2010 – Quiz 3

Live Session: Exercise 1

Rapid Review

Jeopardy

Question displays on the screen, first participant to press buzzer is allowed to answer. Correct answer receives 1 point.

Questions:
1. Q:
   A:
2. Q:
   A:
3. Q:
   A:

Live Session: Exercise 2
Scenario
You've styled your documenting using Word's heading styles and you want to insert a TOC at the beginning of the document that you can continuously update. How can you accomplish this?
Live Session Exercise 3
You need to get a document out the door quickly, and the headings aren't styled. How can you quickly insert a TOC?

Start with objectives and then build a course around it. Think through which things work best in the Individual Space and which things belong in the Group Space.

Once the outline of the course is done, the course designer must then turn their attention to each lesson within the course. When utilizing Flipped Learning, the following lesson plan template can be used as a guide.

Figure 6.2 Flipped Class Lesson Plan Template

Individual Space	
• Pre-Work	
• Notetaking Handout	
Group Space	
• Activity 1	
• Activity 2	
Sample Class Timetable	
Before Training	Check trainee responses via online tool
10 min	Questions from Flipped Video
20 min	Activity 1
15 min	Activity 2
5 min	Closing Activity and reminder to set-up for next training session

HOW DO YOU DETERMINE WHAT GOES IN THE INDIVIDUAL SPACE VS. THE GROUP SPACE?

Many trainers struggle with determining what parts of a lesson are best suited for the Individual Space and which parts should be placed in the Group Space. One mistake we have seen is too much being placed in the Individual Space. We recommend that trainers use Bloom's Taxonomy as a guide. The Individual Space should access lower levels of cognition (knowledge and understanding), and the higher levels of Bloom's should be reserved for the Group Space. When Carrie Kirby and Crystal Fernandes-Harris are teaching new software to their law, the Individual Space work is a series of videos on how to use the software. The Group Space is reserved for one of several activities: practice using the software with the experts present, discussions with peers about best practices, presenting scenarios with problems that need to be solved, or review of key concepts that may have been addressed a couple of weeks ago. All of these Group Space activities access the upper reaches of Bloom's Taxonomy, including application and analysis.

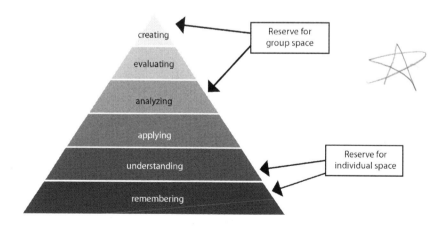

Figure 6.3 Blooms

HOW MUCH SHOULD YOU INVEST IN THE INDIVIDUAL SPACE?

Should you spend significant time and money on developing the pre-learning activities, or is it okay to create the objects in-house? As we interviewed corporate trainers for this book, responses ran the full gamut from in-house/low budget creators to full-blown video production which had Hollywoodish overtones.

Cathy Mongeau, a digital learning design manager at AbbVie Pharmaceutical, is developing a Flipped Training course for a new oncology drug which is about to go to market. Her salespeople need to be experts on all aspects of this new drug. For her pre-learning, she hired a professional film company to create a series of videos with a storyline. Essentially, the videos follow a family member of someone suffering from this form of cancer, and they follow them from diagnosis through treatment. The videos have a Netflix feel with a compelling story and emotional connections, and each section ends with a cliff-hanger. She did not disclose to us the total budget for this course, but we can imagine that it was on the high end.

In the same interview, Cathy also shared how her team built another course where her in-house team simply created the Individual Space objects with virtually no budget. This course, though important, had a limited budget. The interesting thing she shared was that in her opinion, the low-budget course might have been just as effective as the higher budget production.

Freddie Batista, whom we met earlier, develops flipped courses for many of his clients. His clients are diverse, as he works with both call centers and emergency personnel training. He said, "Companies don't understand how long it takes to build a course: they don't take it as seriously as they should." Batista goes on to say that if he is going to build quality into the Individual Space, then it will take many hours, specialized expertise, and great planning. This, of course, requires a budget and dedicated staff.

Crystal Fernandes-Harris and Carrie Kirby from the Day Pitney law firm have both created their own learning objects and have outsourced the creation. Some of the vendor products would have trainees doing things one way and then marking students wrong if they did the same action differently. This frustrated them because, as is often the case with software, there are many ways to achieve the same result. When asked how they decided whether to do their own work or to outsource they said, "It all depends on budget and time."

Another benefit we hear from virtually every trainer we talked to was that when trainers created their own objects, the trainer-trainee relationship was enhanced. The trainer had instant credibility when they were face-to-face with trainees because they already saw the trainer as the expert.

The big takeaway from this section is that you don't have to spend a fortune developing amazing learning objects. Often the reality of time and money will dictate what you can do. Clearly, having a budget and a trained staff of designers and technologists is ideal, but you might not live in that world. It is fine—and sometimes even preferable—to make do with what you have. Don't let the budget get in the way of flipping your training.

BUILD QUALITY LEARNING OBJECTS

Hear us carefully: we don't recommend that you produce sub-par learning objects. Almost all the trainers we spoke with told us that simply having a PowerPoint loaded onto a site was insufficient. People expect more. In a culture of high-gloss digital media and short attention spans, trainees need a brief but compelling experience in which they can connect to both the content and a person. Most found video to be the best way to meet these goals. The videos can have high production values, or they can simply be a compelling screencast. Whichever you choose, create the highest quality objects budget and time will allow.

David Sternela of AbbVie pharmaceutical was given a project to upgrade an existing course on statistics, epidemiology, and risk management. Before taking over the project, the course was getting about 700 hits per month. When David took over the project, he realized that the learning objects needed upgrading. He used Articulate Storyline to create an engaging, interactive, and immersive experience and the number of hits jumped to 2100 per month. Sternela embraced the idea of quality objects. He didn't have a huge budget or a production staff (he was the production staff), but by increasing the quality, trainees were significantly more engaged.

LENGTH OF FLIPPED VIDEOS

In a typical face-to-face training where the trainer "teaches," the presentation of material often can be long and protracted. We have all sat through a boring, seemingly endless PowerPoint presentation. When implementing a Flipped Training model, it is important to keep the learning objects short and focused. It is better to have more modules that are shorter than fewer, longer modules. Tom Phelps, Training and Development Specialist at Fish and Richardson, likes to begin each course with a five- to seven-minute introductory video, and he follows this up with videos that are no longer than two minutes each.

Brian Pitts, who trains physicians at the University of California at Davis Medical School, analyzed how medical students watched video. He observed that students would stay engaged for the first ten minutes and then trail off. He also noted that the many students watched the videos at one and a half times speed. Cathy Mongeau from AbbVie Pharmaceutical used ten- to fifteen-minute videos, and when she surveyed her trainees, they told her they were too long.

I have often heard from trainers that they think there is no way they can take the content of a 45-minute face-to-face training and compress it into a short video. After training thousands of people in flipped methodologies, I have learned that it can be done. Typically, trainers' first videos are about half the length of face-to-face presentation, and with practice, we have seen most trainers cut the ratio to one third. My videos started out at 15–25 minutes, and as I honed the craft of video production, I was able to get the content down to 8–12-minute videos. And if the content trainees need is longer, I recommend that you break the training up into smaller, bite-sized pieces.

BUILD IN INTERACTIVITY

It is not simply good enough to create videos which will be passively watched. Instead, designers must build interactivity into the objects. The goal is for trainees to interact with the content, which then sets them up for a more engaging face-to-face experience.

Below are some techniques trainers can use to increase interaction. Some of the tools are low-tech, requiring nothing

except pencil and paper, and some are more advanced
digital tools which track and measure student engagement.

- Advanced Organizers: This could be as simple as
  a fill in the blank "guided notes sheet," a template,
  a binder with questions, or a page with all the
  necessary charts and problems. Some trainers will
  even place a QR code on the handout which will
  take trainees directly to the flipped video.

- 3-2-1 Strategy: In this strategy, trainees record
  three things they learned from the video, two
  questions about the content of the video, and one
  lingering question they still have. During class
  trainees report the three things they learned,
  interact with each other about the two questions,
  and share with the trainer the one thing they did not
  understand. And if trainees feel they grasped the
  content, they list a takeaway that summarizes their
  learning.

- Assessment Tools: There are many ways to acquire
  direct student feedback from a flipped video. Tools
  such as Google Forms, online assessment suites,
  and most learning management systems have
  quizzing features which allow the trainer to get
  immediate feedback on learning.

- Assessment Tools in the Videos: Many new online
  services contain tools that can insert questions
  within the flipped video. The video will pause
  and ask each trainee to respond to a question or
  prompt. Trainers have access to analytics which
  allows them to know who watched the video, how
  long each student watched the video, and which

questions they answered correctly. These services can also provide discussion forums about the video.

- Interactive Elements besides Questions/Quizzing: The technology of e-learning tools is amazing, and course designers can make use of interactions that can include: hover, drag and drop, click on a region, hands-on with a software tool, etc. These sorts of interactions add to the value of the Individual Space work.

One caution: Don't add an interaction for the sake of adding an interaction. Make sure that the interaction will add to the course and help the trainee advance in knowledge.

There is no one way to build in interactivity. And there is no one tool which is best for every teacher. Finding what works best in any class depends on many factors, and each trainer must find the right mix of interactive techniques, tools, and systems.

TEACH TRAINEES HOW TO WATCH FLIPPED VIDEOS

Watching an instructional video is different than watching a video for entertainment. Trainees inherently understand how to watch the latest superhero movie, but they often need to be taught how to watch instructional content. We liken the difference to learning to read a textbook rather than a novel: it is a skill that must be taught. Ideally, trainers should take a little time in the introduction to the course to teach trainees how to interact with the content. Tom Phelps of Fish and Richardson starts each course with a longer video in which he spends time explaining about Flipped Learning and how trainees can ideally interact with the content. This necessarily makes for a longer introductory video, but it has proven an effective tool to make sure the trainees get the most out of the course.

One technique that has worked in some training settings is a three-step model where trainees watch the video twice and answer questions at the end:

Step 1: Watch, Listen, & Process. Trainees watch, listen, and process the information on the video. They are encouraged not to take notes, but to watch and absorb.

Step 2: Pause and Write. Trainees write down what they've seen on the video. This ensures that they have another opportunity to process what they've just seen as they transcribe the video. Also, they now have a record of their learning to refer to during practice in the face-to-face training.

Step 3: Accountability. Trainees answer a few questions after the video is done. This is typically done in the company's learning management system and provides context and information for increasing the value of the face-to-face training.

PRINCIPLES OF GOOD DIGITAL DESIGN

Richard Mayer has done extensive research on multimedia learning and how people learn best when presented with multimedia. He summarizes the research on multimedia with twelve principles. These principles are being applied to flipped videos, but they apply to any multimedia learning objects. Our (italicized) comments follow the definitions.

1. Coherence Principle—People learn better when extraneous words, pictures, and sounds are excluded rather than included. *Keep your Individual Space objects simple and focused. Too much detail can detract from learning. You don't want to overload learners.*

2. Signaling Principle—People learn better when cues that highlight the organization of the essential material are added. *Provide outlines for your presentation so that people can clearly follow along with the flipped video.*

3. Redundancy Principle—People learn better from graphics and narration than from graphics, narration, and on-screen text. *If the narrator simply reads text that is already on the screen, this will decrease learning.*

4. Spatial Contiguity Principle—People learn better when corresponding words and pictures are presented near rather than far from each other on the page or screen. *Incorporate text next to graphics on the screen.*

5. Temporal Contiguity Principle—People learn better when corresponding words and pictures are presented simultaneously rather than successively. *If there is a voice, it should be synchronized with what is happening on the screen. Time between words and pictures should be avoided.*

6. Segmenting Principle—People learn better from a multimedia lesson is presented in user-paced

segments rather than as a continuous unit. *Keep your videos short.*

7. Pre-training Principle—People learn better from a multimedia lesson when they know the names and characteristics of the main concepts. *If new terms are being introduced, the flipped video will be more effective if there is some "cheat sheet" for learners to refer to.*

8. Modality Principle—People learn better from graphics and narrations than from animation and on-screen text. *Narration is better than having text simply on the screen.*

9. Multimedia Principle—People learn better from words and pictures than from words alone. *Add text to any images in your flipped videos.*

10. Personalization Principle—People learn better from multimedia lessons when words are in conversational style rather than formal style. *Don't be stiff. Be yourself.*

11. Voice Principle—People learn better when the narration in multimedia lessons is spoken in a friendly human voice rather than a machine voice.

12. Image Principle—People do not necessarily learn better from a multimedia lesson when the speaker's image is added to the screen.[1]

I created a simplified version of this when I was first pioneering Flipped Learning in the K-12 space. Below is my list of the top eleven things you should keep in mind when creating flipped videos.

1. Keep Videos Short.

2. Animate Your Voice. It is easy to have a flat voice when recording a video, especially if it is being done in front of your computer in your office. You MUST bring energy and animation to your voice.

3. Work with a Partner. If possible, have two trainers interacting together on the video.

4. Add Appropriate Humor. Trainees will be more engaged when elements of fun are introduced.

5. Audio Matters. If you are recording your video, make sure your audio is clean and understandable. It may seem counterintuitive, but good audio is more important than good video in a video.

6. Don't Waste Your Trainee Time. Keep the videos focused. Going off-topic is only going to waste trainee time.

7. Less Text, More Pictures. Since many trainings start as a PowerPoint deck, many trainers tend to simply go through their text-heavy slides. Video is a visual medium; hence, pictures are more important than text. Err on the side of more pictures. The text should instead be the script that is read, and the slide should be simple and clean.

8. Annotations. Draw on the screen as much as possible. This adds interest, draws attention to key points, and breaks up a slide.

9. Video Clips. If the primary method of creation is a screencast, then splice in video clips of other interesting or relevant material into the screencasts. For example, a video clip of a fireman tying a knot in a PowerPoint about knots.

10. Picture-in-Picture. People like to know whom they are learning from. Many software tools can add a trainer's webcam onto a screencast. Personalizing the learning in this way makes the flipped video more authentic. (This may seem like a contradiction to Mayer's Image Principle, but his research only applied to a static image of the teacher appearing in the multimedia).

11. Questions. Use some sort of technology tool to add questions into the flipped video. These questions can happen inside of the flipped video or could be placed at the end.

OTHER TOOLS BESIDES VIDEO

Flipped Learning has generally been associated with training videos. Though the clear majority of trainers utilize video in a Flipped Training environment, Flipped Learning is not about the videos. The heart of Flipped Learning is a reversal of the Individual and Group Space. With this in mind, there are many other mediums whereby trainees can get work done in the Individual Space. The question you should ask is: What is the best medium for presenting the "easy stuff," or, rather, the lower levels of Bloom's Taxonomy, to trainees?

Reading

Often the best way to get exposed to new material is through text. Short articles, long articles, or even books have worked for generations. Reading may feel like a lost art, but most people can read much faster than they can listen. The average adult can read at a rate of 200 to 250 words per minute (Bailey, 1996), whereas they can listen comfortably at 100 to 150 words per minute (Williams, 1998). Clearly, reading has advantages over video in some instances. One way to enhance reading using digital tools is to use tools that build interaction into the reading. Several available tools will track the number of minutes someone is reading and even have built-in questions and links which can provide data to the trainer about what a trainee did or didn't understand while reading. We will discuss more of this in the technology chapter.

Audio Files

Besides video- and text-based learning objects, audio files can have a significant impact in a training environment. One advantage of audio files is that they are more easily integrated into the daily life of employees, who could use time during their commute, for example, to listen to the files. Bill McGrath, who teaches future Emergency Medical Technicians, uses audio files to teach and finds levels of engagement high.

Online Simulations

Online simulations create a place for trainees to try things out before they are required to attempt them in their job capacities. Many of these simulations are gamified and have both social and skill-building aspects. Simulations are many and varied. Some simulations are simply software practices while others are more complex. We have seen simulations which model things from data analytics to motivational interviewing. There are some companies whose sole purpose is to create and distribute quality online simulations for training. A few notable companies in this space are Forio (Forio.com), Designing Digitally (designingdigitally.com), and Gamelearn (game-learn.com). There are also authoring tools such as ITYStudio (itystudio.com) and Unity (Unity3d.com), which allow trainers to design their own online simulations. Typically, the online simulations should occur in the Individual Space, but there are instances where moving the simulations into the Group Space might be advantageous. It depends upon the amount of group time available, the depth of the simulation, and the objectives of the course.

Other Ways to Interact with e-Learning Objects

Besides videos and reading, there are many online modules that have a variety of different interactions. Online modules can have drag-and-drop options, hot-spot interactions, or hover interactions. Each of these types of interactions has a place when done well. What's important is that each interaction has a purpose. Ask: does this enhance the learning experience for trainees? Too often we have seen these types of interactions embedded into a program to make it glitzy, yet serving little educational purpose.

IDEAL TIME BETWEEN INDIVIDUAL AND GROUP SPACE

In 2013, researchers at York and Santa Clara University asked university students to learn twenty Swahili-English word pairs. There were four groups:

- Group One learned the words and were given an immediate test afterward

- Group Two learned the words in the morning and then took a memory test

- Group Three learned the word pairs in the evening, had a night of sleep and took a test 12 hours later.

- Group Four had twenty-four hours between learning and the test.

When the groups were tested, there was virtually no difference in their scores. However, the study went on to examine long-term retention and checked back with all participants after ten days. Those results were astounding. The longer the spacing between learning and testing, the greater the long-term retention. Remarkably, though, the difference between groups Two and Three was also interesting in that though both of them had a 12-hour interval between learning and the test, the participants that had a sleep cycle between sessions performed better.[2]

This study is one of many on the effect of sleep on long-term retention, and the implication is clear. It is best to have trainees exposed to the introductory material, sleep on it, and then practice it later if long-term retention and change are desirable.

INSERTING QUESTIONS

One of the best ways to build interactivity into a lesson is to insert questions into a flipped video. The questions can serve a variety of purposes, including checking trainee understanding, guiding trainees with content acquisition, and progress monitoring for trainers.

The Value of Questions

In a flipped video, the questions can either be sprinkled throughout the video or placed at the very end. A recent study by psychologist Dr. Henry Roediger of Washington University in St. Louis compared the effect of questions in a flipped video. There were three groups:

- Group One had no questions asked.

- Group Two had questions interspersed throughout the video. The video paused and then students had to answer the questions.

- Group Three had questions at the end of the video.

When the students were tested six weeks after the learning, there was little difference between those who had questions interspersed and those who had questions at the end of the video. However, those with no questions at all scored significantly lower on total retention.[3] The obvious point is that questions add great value to the learning process.

The Type of Questions

One challenge many designers make when putting questions into a flipped video is to determine what level of question difficulty to place in the video. Generally, knowledge and understanding questions vis-à-vis Bloom's Taxonomy are best. This allows trainees the ability to check for understanding and helps with critical recall. Using Bloom's Taxonomy as a guide is, in general, a good rule of thumb.

We suggest an open-ended question be inserted toward the end of the video. Assuming the question is submitted electronically, this allows the instructor to look over the answers to the question and get a good feel for the level of trainee understanding and engagement on the topic. Examples of open-ended questions might include:

- What do you not understand from this video?

- What is one thing you think you will struggle with when applying this to your job?

- How do you see this training impacting your day-to-day function in our company?

Often, the questions trainees ask reveal misconceptions and can both inform a better use of the Group Space time and also provide feedback for retooling the flipped video to make it clearer and more on point.

Chapter 7

Designing Flipped Lessons in the Group Space

The magic of Flipped Learning happens during the Group Space time. Creating engaging Individual Space learning objects is important, but it pales in significance to creating engaging face-to-face activities. Recall that Group Space

Is the time when all the trainees are together with the instructor in the same physical or virtual space. Also, recall that the goal of the Group Space time is to access higher orders of Bloom's Taxonomy. Most trainers utilizing Flipped Learning found a greater deal of challenge in designing meaningful learning activities in the Group Space. Group Space time is critical to any Flipped Learning course. In fact, you can't call it Flipped Learning unless there is some sort of synchronous Group Space time. One common

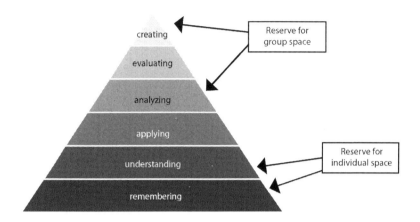

Figure 7.1 Bloom's Taxonomy

mistake I have seen is that trainers focus so much on creating Individual Space learning objects that they forget to revitalize the Group Space time. One trainer even admitted to us that they repeated the Individual Space training during the Group Space time. They were frustrated and were considering scrapping the program. Since they had not really re-designed the Group Space, their Flipped Learning course was doomed to failure.

As stated earlier, Flipped Learning can be considered the operating system of learning, and the different types of learning modalities are apps that can, and should, be utilized during the Group Space time. The focus of this chapter will thus highlight a variety of things you can do in the Group Space. This is not an exhaustive list, nor is every idea on the list best in every context. We recommend that you take these suggestions, find which ones resonate in your context, modify them to meet your needs, and then start trying them out. Many of these strategies have entire books dedicated to them, and if a specific strategy makes great sense in your context, I encourage you to go out and find the books and master these amazing Group Space methodologies. The list of Group Space learning "apps" we will address are represented by Figure 7.2 below.

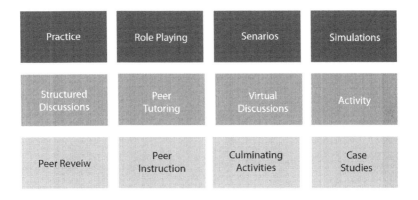

Figure 7.2 Group Space Strategies

WHAT TO EXPECT FROM THE INDIVIDUAL SPACE

Before we go too much further in this chapter, it is critical to understand the expected outcomes from the Individual Space. Many trainers assume that trainees will come into the Group Space with the concepts or processes mastered. This expectation sets a training course up for failure. What realistically happens during the Individual Space time is that trainees are exposed to the content, and many will have only a rudimentary understanding. Trainers who don't plan for this will be frustrated in the Group Space. Realize that many trainees will need some additional support and may come to the Group Space with misconceptions. When designing Group Space activities, it is imperative that you build in time for questions, clarification, and review.

However, don't make the mistake of going over the entire Individual Space lesson, as this will ruin any chance of a successful Flipped Learning implementation.

A TYPICAL TRAINING SESSION TIMELINE

Face-to-face training time comes in a variety of time formats. Group Space time could be one hour or an entire week. Let's examine a typical one-hour course.

Traditional Training		Flipped Training	
Activity	Time	Activity	Time
Warm-Up Activity	5 min	Warm-Up Activity	5 min
Lecture	40 min	Q & A on Flipped Video or Reading	10 min
Guided and independent practice/Group-Space Work	10 min	Guided and independent practice/Group-Space Work	45 min

Figure 7.3 Traditional vs. Flipped Training Timeline

Note the time gained for Group Space work in a flipped training model. The biggest benefit of flipped training is the time recovered to go deeper, practice more, and apply.

When you have longer term courses that might last a week or more, it is important to chunk them into individual lesson timelines like you see above. If training lasts a week, make sure to provide time for Individual Space work for trainees. Build that time into your schedule. Possibly give trainees one hour after lunch to prepare for the next day's workshops or have them start the day with Individual Space time.

PRACTICE

One obvious use of face-to-face class time is to give time for trainees to practice skills. The team from AbbVie Pharmaceutical uses Group Space time to have their sales staff read lab reports. Freddie Batista uses Group Space time for future firemen and firewomen to learn knot-tying and to practice rescue skills. Many flipped trainers also use face-to-face time for practicing how to use the software specific to their organizations. Skills practice in a safe and supervised space where an expert is there to help has proven to be a highly productive use of face-to-face class time. Too often, too little training time is dedicated to this most basic instructional method.

To encourage additional practice, Crystal Fernandes-Harris and Carrie Kirby from Day Pitney created a series of challenges for the employees going through their training. If they successfully completed the challenges, they earned "Day Pitney Dollars ($DP)." Employees could trade in their Day Pitney dollars for gift cards, books, pens, etc. This incentive program was designed to engage learners after the Group Space and worked well for many employees. Many formed groups who worked on the challenges together.

PEER TUTORING

Like practice, peer tutoring seems an obvious use of Group Space time. If trainees are in the same room working together, it is beneficial to have them work in groups. The groups can be assigned by the trainer, or you can allow groups to naturally form. Most learners enjoy working through things with other people, especially when other learners are learning alongside them. As with all things, some trainees will grasp concepts or procedures faster than others, and if they are willing, they can enhance their own learning by helping teach others what they have just learned. Many studies have concluded that if somebody knows they must teach someone else, their learning increases. Of course, caution should be exercised here in that if a trainee with only meager understanding of the material teaches someone else, they may inhibit the learning of the new trainee.

RENAME YOUR "CLASS TIME"

When a trainee hears the term class, they may associate it with sitting and listening to somebody talk at them. Crystal Fernandes-Harris and Carrie Kirby from Day Pitney decided to call their Group Space time a Learning Lab. This simple semantic change conveyed to their employees that the purpose of the time was for practice, play, and application. Get creative and think about something that coveys what you want to accomplish during the Group Space time and have it sound fun, lively, and engaging.

ROLE PLAYING, CASE STUDIES, AND SCENARIOS

When you are interested in working with non-routine solutions to problems or accessing the highest orders of Bloom's Taxonomy, role playing, case studies, and scenarios are excellent ways to use the group learning space. Each technique has three main components:

1. Set Up/Introduction: Trainees need to learn about the scenario, the case study, or the role they will play.

2. Enter the Activity: Dive into the scenario, look into the case-study, or enter into the role.

3. Debrief: The critical aspect of these types of activities.

Role Playing

Role playing is when trainees enter into a role and act as if they are someone else. Role play often leads to emotional connections and, when done well, is a very powerful learning modality. AbbVie Pharmaceutical uses role playing for its sales staff, who need to be experts on the diseases their drugs treat. One of the trainees plays the role of a doctor and another the drug representative, and they role-play the interaction. Other trainees watch the role play, and as a group, they evaluate the session. After each session, the roles rotate to other trainees.

Patty Evans from Yardi, the property management software company, has a unique way she uses role playing. Since all of Yardi's clients use Yardi software, all employees will invariably be asked about some features or tips to use their tools effectively. In this way, every Yardi employee is a teacher. Most of her Group Space time happens in virtual rooms, and she has one trainee explain to another how to use a specific feature of their software. They then evaluate how the teaching session went, and then repeat with a different trainee. They call these role playing activities "Teach Backs" and have found them highly successful in preparing employees for the real questions that clients will pose when they are back at their desks.

When setting up a role play, we suggest a few guidelines which will enable trainers to maximize your group learning time:

- Have clear instructions. Have an information sheet available which specifically gives trainees the necessary background, what role they are being asked to play, what emotions they might be experiencing and the context of the situation.

- Provide sufficient background. Role playing is only as effective as the depth of knowledge a trainee has going into the solution.

- Provide quality feedback. Role playing without feedback is a waste of time since the point of the exercise typically is to improve the quality of an interaction. Many trainers solely rely on trainees to give feedback, but this can be problematic because trainees are not experts and may not be able to give useful feedback. Feedback must be specific and address the key points of the exercise.

- Encourage peer feedback. Peer feedback can be effective if there are clear guidelines as to the type of feedback that trainers are expecting. This should be included ahead of time for observers so that they know what to look for.

- Be careful with assessment. Don't just use role-playing as a final assessment in a training program. If it is going to be used as an assessment, then make sure trainees have time to practice role-playing before the assessment.

- Bring in others. Since trainees are usually unfamiliar with the content, it can be helpful to bring in experts to role play with trainees. Some companies may even hire actors and actresses who have been trained in the specific role you want them to play.

- Allow for emotion. Role playing can often become emotional as trainees embrace their role. As the role play progresses, trainers need to monitor trainees to make sure they don't veer too far afield of the intended purpose of the role play. Have a code word trainees can use to exit the role-play at any time.

Case Studies

A case study is a report about a person, a situation, or a group. Case studies are typically real-world situations; however, for training, case studies can be made-up. Since these represent real-world situations, trainers may soon find that it is important to make the study as real as possible. When presenting the information, don't give trainees only relevant information, but also include irrelevant information. This more closely mirrors the real world in that trainees will need to filter out information they may not necessarily need to interact with the case.

When using a case-study, trainers typically present the case to students, who then have a deep discussion around what happened, why the people in the case made the decisions they did, and how things could be improved or changed. In a Flipped Training environment, the same basic principle applies with a few twists. Instead of the trainers presenting the case study in the group learning space, they present the essence of the case in the Individual Space. This is done either via a reading or a short video which students will interact with before the class session.

During class, the Group Space is dedicated to a rich discussion about the case. One powerful way to maximize the Group Space time is to not share the entire case-study with trainees during pre-learning. Instead cut the case study short and withhold the outcome of the case. Then use

Group Space time to have trainees discuss and share what they would or would not do given the case before them. After a robust discussion, share the end of the case and what happened.

I worked with a CEO who does leadership training for MBA students. In one instance, the CEO used a case study from his own experience as his company was deciding whether to launch a specific product. This was a leadership course, and the CEO wanted his students to wrestle with the hard decisions that leaders must make. For the lesson, he produced a short flipped video about the launch and shared all the information he and his team considered for the product launch. In class, he asked: Should we launch this product given the information shared on the flipped video? A rousing and emotional discussion ensued about the merits of launching. Some students felt they should launch while others were more cautious. Only after the discussion did the CEO tell his students the decision his team made and the results. In case you're wondering, his team decided to launch, and it was a disaster. They should have either held off the launch or gone back to the drawing board. But this created a great learning experience for the MBA candidates and modeled decision making.

Below is a summary of the key tips for planning the best flipped case study.

- Don't share the whole case with the students in Individual Space. Simply give them the information and, like the MBA story above, withhold the rest of the story until the end.

- Have a detailed description. In the description of the case make sure to include all the players, details about the company, an outline of the problem, and any additional information they may need.

- List the resources available. What resources did they have to make a decision or to determine an outcome?

- Identify the complexities. Share the nuances of the situation so trainees can have the most robust discussion possible.

- Have a clear goal. What do you want trainees to discuss, debate, or determine? Be clear.

Case studies can be a very good way to spend class time. Finding or creating quality case studies is hard work, but when done well, this method of using Group Space time can be very useful.

Scenarios

A scenario is simpler than a case study and is often manufactured and not completely real. It is an ideal strategy for novice learners who are starting to analyze a new situation. Often the parameters are less, and there is little or no irrelevant information present. In many ways, a scenario is just a simpler form of a case study. So besides the suggestions mentioned above, a scenario should have the following characteristics:

- Make it relevant. Connect the scenario to the real job you want employees to do.

- Keep it simple. A simple scenario allows you to isolate specific outcomes.

- Don't give too much detail. The purpose is for trainees to get in and out and not have too much irrelevant information. If you are using characters, don't give them too much personality as this can distract learners.

- Always debrief. A well-designed scenario without debriefing can often lead to misunderstanding, misconceptions, and incomplete understanding.

Scenarios can also be done in the Individual Space. There is a growing body of e-learning scenario builders, which often have decision trees built in whereby a student interacts by answering questions. Different outcomes occur depending on how they answer those questions.

SIMULATIONS

A simulation is a virtual medium which imitates the real world. Simulations come in a range from very realistic—as in a flight simulator—to more contrived, where trainees take over the fictional finances of a company and see the effects of their decisions. Since simulations are virtual, there is some debate in flipped circles about whether to introduce them in the Individual Space or the Group Space. This is why we discuss simulations in both chapters.

The discriminator to determine where something fits in a Flipped Training setting is that lower-level cognitive tasks (in Bloom's Taxonomy, knowledge or understanding) fit best in the Individual Space and application and above fit in the Group Space. Since a simulation is usually an application-level activity, it is best done in the Group Space. One benefit of doing simulations in the group learning space is that when learners confront new situations or decisions, the expert teacher or trainer is there to offer direction.

There are many benefits to simulations that make sense in many corporate training contexts:

- Simulations are ideal if the task is dangerous or the stakes are high. It is much better to crash a flight simulator than an actual plane. Or, less dramatically, it is better to anger a virtual customer than a real one. Simulations offer a safe place to make mistakes.

- Simulations can be "played" over and over and usually allow for many iterations of complex events.

- Simulations offer consistent feedback to participants.

- Well-designed simulations can be engaging and fun.

Some types of training are better suited to simulations than others. Simulations are especially useful if the object of the training is to perform under pressure, work with situations which require trainees to connect multiple systems, or navigate situations where employees need to juggle multiple tasks at the same time.

One danger of simulations can be that they can become too "gameish." There certainly are a lot of benefits to gamifying learning, but too often the importance of the game takes too dominant a role, and the actual learning objectives suffer. Make sure that your simulation is tightly focused on the specific objectives of the training.

Many of the trainers we interviewed for this book shared how they use simulations in their training. AbbVie Pharmaceutical created a virtual hospital where people could interact in a virtual setting. EMS trainers use dummies to practice certain health skills. Call center trainees make simulated calls before they work with real customers. And the list goes on.

Again, like other forms of learning, it is critical to take the time to debrief and reflect on the learning with trainees. Questions like, "What would you have done differently, what did you learn, or who was most impacted by X?" can be used to make sure that a simulation is reflected on and the learning maximized.

STRUCTURED DISCUSSIONS

One of the best ways to access deeper-order thinking about a topic is to have rich discussions. However, leading a discussion can often be challenging. Many discussions can easily turn into a rehashing of previous information instead of a deeper dive. When planning a discussion, it is important to be able to answer the question, "What is the purpose of the discussion?" Discussions typically fall into two categories: Discussion for understanding and discussion for deepening. In the book *Questioning for Classroom Discussion*, Jackie Acree Walsh and Beth DankertSattes call these two forms of questioning, questioning for recitation and questioning for discussion.[1] The purposes of these types of questioning are different and have different techniques, as shown in Figure 7.3.

Questioning for Recitation	Questioning for Discussion
To develop foundational knowledge and skills	To extend or deepen thinking
To provide practice	To deepen understanding of concepts by questioning and making new connections
To check for understanding by generating feedback for trainer and trainee	To listen in order to understand
	To reflect on one'sown beliefs
These goals apply to both types of questions To encourage student self-assessment To cue students on what's important to know To encourage student talk (not teacher).	

Figure 7.3 Structured Discussions

*Adapted from Questioning for Classroom Discussion (2015) by Jackie Acree Walsh and Beth DankertSattes (Adapted with Permission, ASCD 2017)

QUESTIONING STRATEGIES FOR UNDERSTANDING:

When questioning for understanding, many educators use the Initiation-Response-Feedback (IRF) loop. A typical interaction might look like one of the following examples.

Example from hair salon styling:

- Trainer: "Which type of hair color highlight would you recommend with this client?"

- Trainee: "I would choose the green highlight because it will accent the client's green eyes."

- Trainer: "Great response. What else would the green highlight accentuate?"

Or, an example from a call center employee:

- Trainer: "With this caller, how would you respond to their belligerent attitude?"

- Trainee: "I will stay calm and direct them to our website for the specific solution."

- Trainer: "My fear is that the caller may feel you don't want to deal with them and they are just being passed on and not heard. Do you have any other ideas about how we could handle this customer?"

Note that in both examples, the trainer follows up with another question that pushes students to understand their product or job more deeply. This form of questioning is especially useful when the goal is for students to understand a specific concept, process, or procedure.

The challenge is to ask good questions, which requires the trainer to plan ahead of time. Questions should not be recall questions, but, instead, questions that push students to probe deeper application or analysis of what they have learned. We have found that it is helpful to put yourself in the place of the learner and remember what it was like to be a novice learner in your field. Another suggestion is to use Bloom's Taxonomy and write out one or two questions at each level appropriate for your lesson. Most find it easier to write knowledge and understanding questions than application or analysis questions.

Instead of just doing an IRF cycle with the whole group, we encourage you to think about having lots of mini-IRF sessions because they will provide trainers more opportunities to interact with trainees. If questions are posed to a whole group, then a trainer can only practice that question once. Asking good initiation and follow-up questions is an art that requires practice to perfect.

When I taught high-school science, I made it a practice to have at least one interaction with each student every day during the group learning time. To manage this, I started class by instructing students to get busy doing an application-level activity. I then roamed the room and spent time having lots of little IRF sessions with small groups of students. These sessions helped me ascertain which students understood key concepts, which students had misconceptions, which ones could move on, and which students needed more remediation.

QUESTIONING STRATEGIES FOR DEEPENING:

In most corporate training, questioning for understanding is all that is necessary. However, there are times when you will want the discussion to go really deep. If you are teaching a leadership class or asking trainees to work with the nuances of often-messy human interaction, then this second kind of questioning is helpful. When engaging in this sort of questioning, instructors will have to give up a certain level of control as much of the class time will be filled with trainee interactions. When done well, this can be a very powerful way to use Group Space time, but when done poorly, it can degrade to a time where people just espouse their own opinions and not much is accomplished.

As in the IRF model, planning is essential when the goal is deeper questioning. Walsh and Sattes posit that there are five stages to effective deep questioning.[2]

Each stage has several requirements. In the following outline, from Walsh and Sattes:

131

1. **Preparing:**

   - Determine one key focus question.

   - Assign students prior work (this should be done in the Individual Space).

   - Consider how you will organize the learning space (the room).

   - Decide how will you structure the discussion (whole class or small group?).

2. **Opening:**

   - Share any norms for the conversation (how often, how long, and how students will back up statements).

   - Pose initial questions.

   - Begin the discussion.

3. **Sustaining:**

   - Sometimes discussions can fizzle unless there is energy to sustain them. If the conversation lags, it is tempting for teachers to inject more questions. Though this is sometimes appropriate, if student interaction is the focus, then sustain the conversation by saying things like, "tell me more . . . ; we are with you, can you expand?" Use nonverbal communication as well by nodding and keeping eye contact.

- Monitor student interaction. Often, conversations can be dominated by a few people. Make sure to get everyone's feedback and thoughts.

4. **Closing:**

- In this stage, trainers can summarize the thoughts of the group and check if their summary reflects what the learners learned. This may include going back to the essential question posed at the beginning of the discussion, or a chance to let students summarize.

5. **Reflection:**

- Margaret Wheatley said, "Without reflection we go blindly on our way, creating more unintended consequences, and failing to achieve anything useful."[3] Allow time for trainees to do some personal reflection.

I often close training sessions with a time of personal reflection using the 5-5-5 model. Each participant is asked to pull out either a pen and paper or a computer and individually write down the answers to the following three questions:

- What will they do in the next five days with what they have learned?

- What will they do in the next five weeks with what they have learned?

- What will they do in the next five months with what they have learned?

A few people then share their reflections. This has proven to be a powerful time both individually and corporately as people commit to change.

Questioning is more art than science. I encourage you to take the time to plan, be willing to give up some control, and enter the messy world of questioning.

PEER INSTRUCTION

Peer instruction is a learning system designed by Eric Mazur, a physics professor at Harvard University. Mazur was dissatisfied with the traditional lecture format and wanted his students to have in-depth understanding of the concepts he teaches. His students learn rudimentary concepts at home and, during class, Mazur takes them through the peer instruction cycle, which comprises the following steps:

1. Instructor poses a question based on students' responses to their pre-class reading.

2. Students reflect on the question.

3. Students commit to an individual answer.

4. Instructor reviews student responses.

5. Students discuss their thinking and answers with their peers.

6. Students then commit again to an individual answer.

7. The instructor again reviews responses and decides whether more explanation is needed before moving on to the next concept.[4]

A good peer instruction exercise involves having higher-order thinking problems with which students struggle together in class. This method has a mixture of individual accountability and group work, which helps students engage and learn deeply. To learn more about peer instruction, we encourage you to read Dr. Mazur's book Peer Instruction: A User's Manual (Pearson, 1996).

PEER REVIEW

Though trainers can give feedback, often peers can provide even better feedback. When directed well, student insight can be powerful both for the one to whom they are giving the feedback and for themselves. Bill McGrath trains EMT professionals and has his students film each other practicing emergency techniques. The students then evaluate each other's videos and discuss how to improve. In a recent conversation with a cardiovascular doctor who trains cardiovascular residents, I learned how the residents were filming each other's techniques in the cadaver room. Like McGrath's students, his students also traded videos, evaluated their peers' techniques, and made suggestions for improvement.

In other fields, you might have a call-center employee rate a call or have a legal assistant watch somebody reorganize a document, or a leader simulate a difficult conversation. Then have peers evaluate the process, activity, or discussion, and use this as a springboard for improving performance for any training. This requires the trainer to relinquish some of the control of the learning and may be harder for some trainers who feel they need to always be in control. We recommend you take a big leap and relinquish some of the control of the Group Space time. We have done this and have been amazed at the results. This is especially powerful with adults who have lots of life experiences and who tend to thrive when they are given more ownership of the learning.

LIVE OR VIRTUAL FACE-TO-FACE SESSIONS?

Deciding whether to have your Group Space time in a live training session or in a virtual room should be made carefully. In some cases, virtual sessions are the only option. It may be unfeasible and prohibitively expensive to bring hourly employees together for training. Or, in the case of Freddie Batista, who trains remote call-center agents whose employers have chosen to eliminate brick-and-mortar call centers, his trainees would have no centralized physical space in which to gather. So all the training for newly onboarded employees—in software interface, company product lines, and customer service principles—has to be done in a virtual Group Space. Certainly, there are times when a virtual, synchronous meeting is all you need, but it can present challenges. Most flipped corporate trainers we talked with struggled more with developing meaningful Group Space activities in virtual versus live sessions. Creative use of face-to-face time is harder when people are sitting in front of a screen. Breakout sessions or having trainees practice when they've learned is much harder to manage in a virtual training environment.

I do encourage you to carefully weigh if your training should be face-to-face in-person or virtually. Some questions you might want to ask yourself are:

- What is the long-term goal of this training program?

- How important is this training for the mission of my company?

- If employees don't get this training, what will be the long-term consequences to my company?

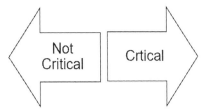

The goal of these questions is to answer one simple question:

How critical is the training? If your training is more on the critical side, we encourage you to invest in face-to-face, in-person training. If the training is more to the non-critical side, it may be better to have a virtual face-to-face meeting.

CONCLUSION

As stated at the outset of this chapter, the magic of Flipped Learning happens in the Group Space. Too many people feel that Flipped Learning is all about the videos. This chapter should serve as a guide to how you can better utilize the group learning space. We encourage you to identify which strategies would work best in your courses and context.

Next up, Errol and I will look at the technology impacting Flipped Learning and give you a blueprint for making great technology decisions.

Chapter 8

The Technology of the Flipped Classroom

One misconception about Flipped Learning is that it is a technological solution to training. The perception is that you must first start with the technology and then follow up with something to do in class. Contrary to this view, Flipped Learning is a fundamentally good educational practice that happens to have a technological component. It is not just for those involved in the e-learning industry, but rather a model that can be adopted by virtually all organizations looking to enhance and transform their training.

That said, there is a technological component to Flipped Learning. Generally, the individual learning space is where the bulk of the technology is used. However, there are some technological tools which can enhance the Group Space as well. This chapter will investigate how to get e-learning objects organized, tools for the Individual Space, and tools for the Group Space. The chapter will conclude with a framework for organizations to decide how to choose the best tools by providing a series of questions and recommendations to consider before selection. Should you use out-of-the-box tools, or should you have tools custom-made? What things should you look out for and what pitfalls should you avoid?

GETTING ORGANIZED — THE LEARNING MANAGEMENT SYSTEM

"The definition of genius is taking the complex and making it simple." —Albert Einstein

Most likely your organization has a learning management system (LMS). An LMS is a place where you can organize all the e-learning objects you will use in the Individual Space. These systems allow you to upload documents and videos and link to online content. Most allow you to include interactive elements such as quizzes and forums. They also allow you to monitor student usage of the system. Many even have video-conferencing built in, allowing for a virtual Group Space meeting room.

But before we delve too deeply into learning management systems, it is important to note that Flipped Training can be done without one. We know of one trainer who used his company's social networking site and blog, YouTube, and Survey Monkey to flip his training. He monitored who watched what and when, and he was able to make it work. You can definitely flip training without an LMS, but it will make your task much easier if you have one.

When designing a course on an online platform, it is important that the design is clean and simple. An LMS can be a bit intimidating to employees who are not used to learning online, and if the online interface is complex, it can lead to ineffective learning on the part of your employees. It may be necessary to spend some time teaching new employees how to navigate your LMS.

If your organization does not have an LMS, we recommend that you choose one that has a simple interface and which meet the needs of your training. We also recommend that you choose only one. We talked with one company that had three different learning management systems, and even had some of the same courses across all platforms. This duplication of work was inefficient and ultimately harmed the training arm of the organization. Employees would sometimes take a course in one learning management system and then another course in a different system. This confused employees because every time they took a new course they had to learn the ins and outs of a different LMS.

There is a wide array of LMSs available which can be used and customized for your organization. Most companies purchase subscriptions to these tools. Some, though, have developed their own LMSs due to the individual needs of their organizations. If you recall, Bill McGrath trains in the EMS and firefighting industry. As he pioneered Flipped Learning in his space, he realized a need for a custom platform for his industry. So, he partnered with the technology platform Blender to create a custom LMS. He feels that the key to the design of the platform was how it emphasized and directed trainees to quality Group Space activities where the EMS and firefighters spent much more time practicing skills and procedures.

Regardless of whether you create your own system, customize one, or simply subscribe to a basic LMS provider, it is vital that you have a single, simple system that meets your needs.

TECHNOLOGICAL TOOLS FOR THE INDIVIDUAL SPACE

In an effective Flipped Training environment, there are a variety of tools that will need to be mastered.

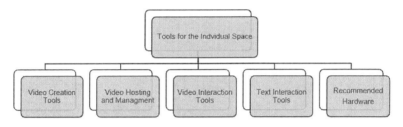

Figure 8.1 Tools for the Individual Space

Video Creation

When people think of Flipped Learning, they think about videos being used in the Individual Space. And though we have learned that Flipped Learning is NOT primarily about the videos, most people do use video in Flipped Training environments. There are a variety of ways organizations create videos for training. Depending on which method you use, different tools will be required.

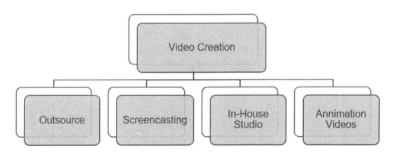

Figure 8.2: Video Creation Options

142

Outsourcing

As we discussed in Chapter 5, it is sometimes effective to hire outside companies to produce content. Typically, this will create the greatest production quality. However, it can sometimes feel cold to the trainees. Refer to Chapter 5 for situations when outsourcing the content makes the most sense.

Screencasting

By far, the most common way trainers create video for Flipped Learning is via a screencast. Screencasting programs record whatever is happening on your computer screen along with audio, and in some cases, a webcam shot. Trainers typically create a lesson or presentation in some sort of presentation software, such as Microsoft PowerPoint, and use a screencasting program to record them teaching through their slide deck. This coupled with digitally drawing over the slide show will enhance the production quality. If the training requires some sort of software demonstration, screencasting is a must.

Screencasting programs exist on all platforms, and there are many vendors that make these sorts of programs. Some programs work only on a PC, others only on a Mac, and others on tablet devices. Below is a partial list of some screencasting programs you may want to check out.

Windows	Macintosh	Tablets
Adobe Captivate	Adobe Captivate	Know Recorder
Articulate Storyline	Articulate Storyline	Explain Everything
Screencast-O-Matic	Screencast-O-Matic	Touchcast
Snagit	Snagit	Show Me
Camtasia		Doceri
Camstudio	Screenflow	Educreations
Office Mix	Apple Quicktime	

Figure 8.3 Screencasting Programs

In-House Production

Several organizations built video studios to increase the production value of their training videos. Brian McGrath, our EMS trainer from the University of California at Davis Medical School, utilized the school's TV production studio and some medical illustrators to increase the production value of his videos.

Most studios utilize green-screen technology and have computers loaded with video editing software tools such as Adobe Premier and Final Cut Pro. One new thing that has caught the attention of the flipped community is lightboard technology. A lightboard, pictured below, is a piece of glass on which the trainer can draw to highlight specific content. With more powerful editing software, images, and videos can be overlaid onto the video.

Figure 8.4 Lightboard Video

Animation Videos

We have all seen the cool video clips in which someone draws quickly on-screen with a voiceover. This is done a lot in advertising. After all, nowhere is the pressure to be extremely engaging in a short period of time greater than in ads. These videos are engaging and can be very effective. There are several companies in this space, including PowToon, VideoScribe, Moovly, and Explee.

Video Hosting and Video Management

Once a video is created, it needs to be uploaded somewhere. Though YouTube may be a good place for K-12 educators, it is usually a bad idea for corporate training. Often the videos created contain proprietary information which needs to be secure. Most, if not all, LMSs allow video uploads. An added benefit is that when you upload to your LMS, it is protected by a password as a part of a company's internal system.

There area number of enterprise video hosting platforms. Advantages of these types of programs are numerous.

Besides providing a secure storage space, most have additional features such as indexing of videos, the ability to search for words in the videos, ways to build questions into or at the end of the videos, screencasting recorders, powerful analytics, and a plethora of other features. Companies in this space include Brightcove, MediaPlatform, Kaltura, VBrick, Panopto, SonicFoundry, Yuja, and KZO Innovations.

Video Interaction

As we discussed in Chapter 5, a best practice in Flipped Learning is that for any given video there are questions and interactions. These tools allow the instructor or course designer to build questions into or after the video. These tools also collect and analyze trainee viewing data, which informs the instruction of the trainer. These interactive elements can be found in a variety of places. All LMSs can ask questions after watching a video. Some LMSs can insert questions into the video. There are also stand-alone video tools which are very adept at tracking and adding questions in the videos. And many of the enterprise video platforms allow for interactions. As with all tools, it is important to find the right tool for your organization. Some of the tools in this space are Adobe Captivate, Articulate Storyline, edPuzzle, PlayPosit, Hapyak and Office Mix.

A similar type of tool has recently emerged where students and trainees can interact with a flipped video by giving video responses. With these tools, the trainee watches a video, and instead of giving a text-based response, they turn on a webcam or use their mobile device to record short video responses to prompts or videos. Flipgrid and Recap are among the first movers in this space.

Text Interaction Tools

As we've discussed, Flipped Learning does not always involve video. Video interaction tools that track and analyze trainee video behavior are not the only interactive option. There are also text interaction tools, which allow the trainer to insert interactive elements directly in the text. Interactive elements include questions, videos, audio files, and commenting. When the trainer views usage statistics, they can view things such as time spent in the document, answers to any questions asked, and comments that the trainee has made. The two tools we have noticed are Inkling and Actively Learn. Note that Actively Learn is very K-12 focused.

Hardware

To create quality flipped videos, there are a few pieces of hardware you may want to utilize. Obviously, there is a need for a computer or tablet, but other accessories have greatly enhanced the production quality of flipped videos.

- Microphones: Most built-in microphones in computers or mobile devices are adequate, but if there is a need for greater audio fidelity, there is a wide variety of USB microphones on the market.

- Drawing Tablets: Annotating on a screencast enhances the viewing experience of trainees. It can also be very helpful when working out problems, highlighting text, or drawing attention to an image. Many computers have a touch screen, and the pen feature is intuitive. However, one problem with using a touch screen is that when using a pen device, the tapping sound is often picked up by the built-in microphone of the computer, which is not ideal.

Another option is to purchase an external tablet input device. These devices typically connect via USB to your computer and are essentially a slate. They are glorified mice, but instead of a mouse interface, they have a pen interface. When I started flipping my chemistry classes in 2007, I feel that it would not have worked had it not been for my external tablet input device. It was critical that I worked out chemistry problems with a pen device. One other advantage of pen input devices is that for the most part, they don't get outdated. I have used the same pen input device for eight years. During those eight years, I went through six computers, and since the pen input device is essentially an enhanced mouse, it kept on working. Though there are many brands of these devices, I am a fan of the tablets made by Wacom.

Figure 8.5 Pen Input Device

Document Camera: Some trainers have found document cameras to be useful for recording if much of your material is either paper-based, or small objects which need to be seen. A document camera is a webcam which points downward. They typically plug into a computer via a USB cable and have a recording feature. Some even have recording capability without having to plug the device into the computer.

Figure 8.6 Document Camera

TECHNOLOGICAL TOOLS FOR THE GROUP SPACE

Not only is the Individual Space enhanced by quality technology tools, but the Group Space can also be enhanced with technology.

Video Conferencing

Many companies' Group Space is not done face-to-face, but rather in virtual rooms. A quality video conferencing tool is a must if you plan for some of your Group Space time to be done virtually. Those trainers we chatted with for this book were using a variety of video conferencing tools including Cisco WebEx, GoToMeeting, GoToWebinar, Skype for Business, Blackboard Collaborate, and Adobe Connect. Some features we like to see in a video conferencing tool intended to replace the Group Space are:

- Intuitive drawing features
- Recording of the sessions
- Small group breakout rooms
- HD video for all participants and presenters
- Student sharing by taking over the main screen
- LTI (Learning Tools Interoperability) integration for tracking and integration
- LMS integration
- Mobile options so that trainees can use any device to connect
- Simple application and file sharing
- Question and answer spaces
- Screen sharing for both the trainer and the trainees
- Chat functions for a backchannel where participants can chat with each other without broadcasting to the rest of the class.
- Robust polling features
- Simple user interface

Assessment Tools

During the group learning time, there is often need to get feedback from trainees. There is a wide variety of technological tools that collect formative feedback from trainees. I have used Plickers when working with organizations. With this tool, each trainee is given a piece of paper with a unique QR code on it. A question is placed on the screen, and trainees respond by holding up their card orientated in one of four ways. The teacher then scans the room with a mobile device, and the results are collected and displayed in real time. Some tools incorporate competition and are fun. Patty Evans from Yardi is a big fan of Kahoot, which adds mild competition and has fun music, which energizes her trainees. Other tools in this space are Quizizz, Socrative, Poll Everywhere, and Mentimeter.

Simulation Software

Simulations can be effective strategies in both the individual and the group spaces. Online simulations take a great deal of time to develop but can be highly effective tools in training. The tool that was most popular with those we interviewed for this book is Articulate Storyline. As with all tools, there are many other simulation software platforms you may want to consider, including Adobe Captivate, Adobe Animate, and Lectora Inspire.

MAKING THE RIGHT TECHNOLOGY DECISIONS

Every technology choice you make represents a life-changing fork in the road. Okay, that's just a bit melodramatic, but not by much. Go down the right technology path, and your training program is on the proverbial yellow brick road to accelerated learning. Go down the wrong path and you, your tech team, and your trainees are on the rocky road to tech hell . . . Arggggh!

Few things can make, break, or accelerate Flipped Learning than the technology choices we make. Yet, while the stories of wrong tech choices have risen to legendary status, the stories of great choices (and how they were made) are largely unknown. Thus, in the following section, we aim to demystify the art and science of choosing the right technology for your training needs. We'll start with the basic considerations and close with the 17 deadly sins to avoid.

RULES OF THUMB

#1 The Basic Four Test: Generally speaking, you've probably made a good technology choice if:

- It works
- It's used
- It scales
- It lasts

These are the four basic measures of good training technology. Technology that doesn't work as expected when expected is rejected by trainees; doesn't grow with your needs, or quickly becomes obsolete is simply not good technology. It may have lots of cool features, employ cutting-edge applications, and come with free car washes and unlimited coffee, but the tech is only good if it works, it's used, it scales, and it lasts.

#2 The Simplicity Test: The simplicity principle is simple:

"Simple technology gets used; technology that is not simple doesn't."

K-12 classrooms are filled with exotic educational tech tools that magically morphed into decorative furniture because they were too complex for practical use.

Over the past year, we surveyed several technology developers who produce educational tech tools with robust features. We asked each one a simple question: How many of the features built into your system are used by subscribers? The typical answer was well below 25 percent.

We've found that the best technology choices are simple and intuitive to use. This, of course, is not exclusive to Flipped Learning. The simplicity principle applies to all technology acquisitions.

#3 The YOU Test: Like trainees, no two training environments are the same, so differentiation and personalization matter in technology selection as well.

As you produce training materials, you'll want to pick the tools that are right for you and your work flow. You'll want to pick the tools that suit your company and its culture. A training director at a high-tech firm is likely dealing with a very different population than a tire factory. Make sure the tools are a good fit for you and your team.

With those basics covered, let's dive head first into the big do's and don'ts of selecting education technology.

THE 17 DEADLY SINS OF EDUCATION TECHNOLOGY SELECTION

Today our relationship with technology is the classic love/ hate story: We can't live with it, and we can't live without it. The L&D graveyards are filled with hardware, software, gadgets, and gizmos from training and technology marriages that died.

At the risk of sounding like a parent raising tough questions about your fiancé, here is a quick rundown of the 17 points you should consider before hooking up with any training technology. Asking these questions can lead to a long and blissful relationship with your training tech. Failing to consider any one of these can be a deadly sin.

#1 Initial Cost

Too often the price listed on the site or touted by the sales rep is not the full cost of running off with that cute new piece of tech. To avoid underestimating the initial cost, there are some key questions you'll want to ask before saying "I do."

Initial Cost Questions:

- Is there an additional set up cost?

- Is there a fee for initial support?

- What other accessories will we need to use the technology?

- What are the costs of these accessories?

- Are there any fees for integrating the technology with my current systems?

- Do we need to hire someone, or will the vendor do the integration?

- If the setup and integration are done in-house, how much time and resources will it cost my organization?

- If customization is needed, are there any customization costs?

- How does the vendor charge? Per user, flat rate per organization, tiered rates?

- Is the solution scalable?

- What is the cost of adding another 10, 100, or 1,000 users?

You should also consider the cost of being too "cost conscious." This goes back to the Basic Four Test. A low-cost solution is only good if, it works, it's used, it scales, and it lasts.

Finally, companies will often offer volume discounts above a certain number of users, subscribers, or volume. Neither the Constitution, local business regulations, nor the Bible prevents you from asking for the discount even if you don't meet the benchmark. Everything is negotiable!

#2 Reliability

Sometimes the notion of "reliable technology" is an oxymoron. A while back, we stumbled onto a discussion in a forum for technologists. One of the members was responding to a poster who expressed deep frustration with software that wasn't performing as expected. The technologist replied philosophically, "Sometimes we expect too much of technology. If you had any idea how many processes have to come together at just the right place and time for this program to function, you would realize that it's a miracle that it ever works."

Fortunately, most of the technologies we use are reasonably reliable. But as our founding fathers wrote, "all technology is not created equal." Okay, we could be wrong about the source of that quote, but whoever said it was right.

When it comes to technology, the potential reliability pitfalls are many:

- Buggy software

- Unstable hardware

- Erratic system interfaces

- Technology produced by poorly funded companies that go belly-up and leave you stranded

- The list goes on

Below are the pivotal questions that can help you avoid the most common reliability pitfalls.

Reliability Questions:

- Have you asked your peers for recommendations?

- Have you asked for references from the vendor you selected?

- Have you checked the online reviews and comments?

- Have you checked the vendor's support forum?

- Have you asked the vendor what tech problem they are currently working to resolve?

- Have you investigated the financial stability of the company? Are they a startup or an established company?

- Have you asked for a trial period?

This is a good time to mention that the amount of due diligence should be proportional to the cost of the acquisition. If there is little at stake in trying the technology, then go for it. But if you're about to sign a $500,000 purchase order, the steps above are well worth the time.

#3 User Friendliness

Let's face it: some technology is created by people who feel and think just like us, but other technologies are designed by aliens from another planet. These creatures think in ways that are fundamentally counterintuitive to the way we think. This is why it's so important to apply the simplicity test.

Great technology is easy to use and easy to figure out without a 200-page user's manual. Simple tech gets used, so doing a pre-purchase simplicity test is critical. Below are the questions to help you avoid getting technology tools that are antisocial to you, your staff, and your trainees:

User Friendliness Questions:

- How long did it take you to get familiar with the tool?

- How intuitive is the tool? Can you figure out the basics without a manual?

- What are online users saying about user friendliness?

- What issues are being posted to the product's user forum?

- Is the technology being broadly recommended?

- Have you given a sample to a non-tech user to try out?

- Have you given the tool to a trainee to try out?

#4 Training Requirements

Some software, hardware, gadgets, and widgets will require some training. You'll want to get a heads up on the learning curve and training costs before you tie the knot. Below are the questions to avoid training pitfalls.

Training Requirements Questions:

- Have you asked the company how much training is required?

- Who will train your staff?

- Is there an additional fee to train the staff?

- Where and how will the training be performed? Onsite, online, a blend?

- What tech skills are needed to use the tool?

- What follow-up or remedial training is available?

#5 Ease of Setup

One of the most beautiful terms in the technology universe is "plug and play." These three words typically mean that all we have to do is unpack it, fire it up, and the technology will work without the need for configuration by the user.

In practice, plug and play works as promised most of the time. Other times, it's more like, "plug, call support, wait for technician, pull out some hair, update your operating system, pull out more hair, download the latest version, reboot the system, and then play."

Another "ease-of-setup" issue involves sign-up. Some cloud-based tools have a one-click sign-up with Facebook or Twitter.

Others have an elaborate process that involves submitting a full dossier on each user, their kids, and three generations down their family tree. The sign-up issue can become even more frustrating when integrating with other tools that also require logins and passwords. Below are the questions that matter.

Ease of Setup Questions:

- Is the tool really "plug and play"?

- Did you test it?

- Does it "just work"?

- Is the tool easy for trainees to sign in to?

- Can the login process be easily integrated?

- Is it easy to mass-migrate data into the tool?

#6 Support

"Houston, we have a problem." These are words that neither NASA nor L&D professionals want to hear when new technology is deployed.

But hey, tech problems come with the territory. So when bad tech happens to good people, what we want is great technology support.

Tech support is like credit: the best time to ask for it is when you don't need it. There are few things more frustrating than discovering that your vendor has a killer, always-available sales team and an "I want to kill them," never-available tech support team.

Below are the right questions to consider.

Support Questions:

- Have you tried calling customer support before deciding to buy the tool?

- Do their tech support hours match your company needs?

- Do they offer multiple modes of support, i.e., phone, email, chat, online forum?

- Are they easy to reach and helpful?

- Do they offer a dedicated support representative?

- Do they maintain a record of your support inquiries?

- Are there training videos on the company website?

- Have you watched some of the training videos?

- Have you asked others about the company's customer support?

#7 Ease of Access

Often we come to technology in different ways. We may access it on a desktop computer, a laptop, or a mobile phone. We may access it from the training room or the shop floor. We may need access from our home office or a rented meeting room at the Hilton in Katmandu. Will your technology be available to you and your trainees at the time and place you need it?

Ease of Access Questions:

- What are my accessibility needs?

- Is the tool set up for single sign-on?

- Do all of my existing systems integrate with the tool?

- Depending on who sets up accounts, is account setup seamless for your staff?

- Is the tool cloud-based or locally installed?

- Is there a single interface for trainer and trainee?

- Is the tool user-friendly from all types of devices (computers, mobile devices, etc.)?

- What is the quality of Internet access required for effective use?

- Do I need offline access?

#8 Versatility

It's crazy when you stop and think about it: You have a phone, camera, computer, map, mailbox, calendar, and boom box in your pocket. If that doesn't blow your mind (or you've never heard of a boom box), you're under 30.

It's really convenient to have all those technologies in one device. Versatility is clearly good, but not always sufficient for all needs. For example, professional photographers still buy insanely expensive cameras because they need more features and flexibility than they get on a cell phone camera. We shot our initial training videos on an iPhone. But when we upgraded, we found that the improvement was stark, and we could never go back.

The same applies to training technology. Below are the questions you'll want to ask when considering multifunction tech.

Versatility Questions:

- Does the tool do more than one thing?

- Do we need a tool that does more than one thing?

- Do we need a specialized tool with more robust features?

- Is the tool multi-platform compatible? (e.g., on computers, Chromebooks, mobile devices?)

#9 Technology Life Cycle

Oh, how sweet it would be if we could find the right technology, buy it, set it up, and forget it forever.

THE TECHNOLOGY OF THE FLIPPED CLASSROOM

Unfortunately, technology stopped working that way on day two. In fact, on the day you buy any technology, somewhere in a hidden bunker at an unknown location, a team of geeks is already working on the next version. It's hard to know when your technology will become obsolete, but planning for the day you'll have to update or replace it is a Jedi Master move.

Technology Life Cycle Questions;

- What has been the update schedule of the technology?

- How essential is it to have the latest version?

- What should I do now to make upgrading or replacing easier?

- How should I budget for obsolescence?

- Who needs to be involved in our update process?

#10 Cultural Compatibility

Cultural compatibility touches many bases. It includes language, gender, geography, age, and technological savvy, to name a few. It would be as foolish to buy overpowered technology for a low-tech staff as it would be to buy dreadfully underpowered technology for a very tech-savvy staff. A virtual company might need more mobile technology than one where all staff is in the same building. Matching technology to culture is vital. The key questions are listed below.

Cultural Compatibility Questions:

- Does the technology suit our cultural needs?

- Does the technology fit our diversity needs?

- Does the technology meet our language needs?

- Does the technology match our generational needs?

- Does the technology fit the staff's education level and tech skill set?

- Does the technology match our company values?

#11 Compatibility with Existing Systems

Forgive us as we geek out for a moment and talk about interoperability, backward compatibility, and information exchange. It's all tech talk for the big question: Will the technology you select get along and play nice with the technology you already have?

How big is this technology compatibility problem? The global systems integration market size was valued at $233.9 billion in 2015 according to Grand View Research.[1] The U.S. market alone is projected to reach $387.85 billion by 2021, according to Markets and Markets.[2]

Suffice it to say that the problem is big enough that if you are making a large technology purchase (and it must work well with technology you already have), it's crucial to bring in someone who can answer the following questions:

Compatibility with Existing Systems Questions:

- Is the new technology compatible with my existing hardware systems?

- Is the new technology compatible with my existing software systems?

- Is the new technology compatible with the other related company systems?

- If the new tech is not compatible, how much of that $387.85 billion will we have to pay to get our systems to play nicely with each other?

#12 Infrastructure Needs/Costs

Infrastructure needs are another murky, dark sinkhole that can appear when you least expect it and gobble up your technology budget. It seems that infrastructure needs go in only one direction—up. That's only somewhat true, as wireless technology has certainly reduced telecommunication infrastructure costs for many companies. Maybe this is an exception; we don't know for sure.

What we do know is that buying new technology can translate into unplanned demand for new infrastructure to support it. You may need more servers, access points, wiring, routers, and all sorts of doohickeys and thingamajigs that you never considered. And bandwidth, in particular, is important in Flipped Training environments since Flipped Learning is video-centric and bandwidth-hogging.

This is another area where we need to call in the Geek Squad to help sort this out. The basic questions are:

Infrastructure Needs/Costs Questions:

- Who needs to be at the table to evaluate our infrastructure needs?

- Does our company have sufficient bandwidth to incorporate this technology?

- Does our company have the right in-house staff to manage the technology?

- Do we have a budget to upgrade our infrastructure?

- Have we factored in the costs of outside consultants and contractors in the upgrade process?

#13 Interactivity

Simply said, when it comes to education and training, interactive technology trumps passive technology. So what do you need to ask?

Interactivity Questions:

- Is the tool interactive?

- Does the tool actually get trainees interacting in the Individual Space?

- Does the tool encourage more in-class interactivity?

#14 Data Privacy

The whole area of data privacy involves a mash-up of competing laws, rules, and interests. The potential conflicts have to be considered and balanced when making technology decisions. The questions:

Data Privacy Questions:

- Who should get access to the information required to use the technology?

- How much access should be granted to various stakeholders?

- What access to company information will the vendor have?

- What is the technology provider's privacy policy?

- Does the technology provider repurpose, sell, or use your submitted data?

- Have you carefully read the provider's privacy policy?

#15 Safety and Security

As we approach the gray area of digital safety and cyber-security, it requires an extra measure of optimism to believe that we can have any control over these issues whatsoever. After all, if the bad guys can hack into banks, military bases, and my antivirus- and firewall-protected laptop, is anything safe? Despite the high-level confessions that digital security is basically out of control, the experts advise us to take basic precautions anyway. So the questions are as follows.

Safety and Security Questions:

- Who should be at the table to discuss tech security issues?

- Should we use closed systems or open systems?

- What security measures does the technology provider employ?

- Does the technology have an online history of security issues?

- What administrator controls does the technology offer?

- How quickly has the technology provider responded to security issues?

- Can user activity be blocked or limited?

- What sort of backup system does the technology employ?

- Did you view the available administrator controls before purchasing?

- What other security measures should we take on our end?

#16 Maintenance Costs

Depending on the type of technology you're considering, there may be some ongoing maintenance costs. On the low end, that can simply involve the time needed to download security updates. On the high end, routine updates can require across-the-board changes to settings, system interfaces, and user policies that may cost time and money to reconfigure on a company-wide scale.

Maintenance Costs Questions:

- What are the known maintenance costs of the technology?

- What has been the maintenance history of this technology?

- Will you need dedicated staff to manage the routine maintenance?

- How are most customers maintaining the technology?

- In the case of hardware, how available and costly are spare parts?

#17 Hidden Costs

Caveat Emptor! Let the buyer beware. Failing to anticipate hidden costs is among the most deadly sins of technology selection. Barely a week goes by in which we don't see some egregious new twist on the concept. We recently used a "free" online resource to draft a document. The document was over ten pages long, and the program did a great job of guiding us through the key questions. Then came the big surprise! We got to the end of the very long process and discovered that putting the information in was free. Printing the information out required payment.

Hidden costs come in all shapes, sizes, and amounts.

Some of the most common include:

- Credit card charges that are automatically triggered by events you didn't know were buried in the terms of use

- Excess usage fees

- "Freemium" models that charge you nothing to begin using the technology but demand a fee for essential features

- Window-dressing warranties and support fees that don't cover any meaningful support

- Technology insurance policies with gaping coverage exceptions

- Legal ransomware that locks you out of your company data if monthly or annual fees are not paid

- And perhaps the most surprising and disruptive, the cost of switching all of your data from a provider that you've decided is too horrific to keep.

Hidden Costs Questions:

- Are there annual fees?

- Are there upgrade fees?

- Is there a support contract?

- If this is a freemium model, to what extent are you committed when you reach a certain level of usage?

- If you buy the software, is there a fee to get support?

- What happens to all my data if we decide to change providers?

- What's involved in making the change to another provider?

The best defense against hidden costs is to ask lots of questions before you buy and check online reviews. Typically, technologies with horrendous hidden costs will have a sizable community of angry past users waving red digital flags to potential users.

Now that we have all of that out of the way let's end on a positive note.

LOOKING AHEAD

We all know that technology (warts and all) is opening amazing new possibilities in training and learning. Virtual reality, artificial reality, and mobile learning are just a few of the rising technology stars.

Now, the tech wizards tell us that Experience API (xAPI), a relatively recent software specification, is opening new frontiers in learning and talent development. It's geeky stuff that includes:

- The ability to operate anywhere, on any device, on any server, outside the web browser

- Maintaining complete control over content delivery and user experience

- Added security to prevent users from cheating

- Team-based e-learning

- Delivery of a richer multi-modal learning experience

- Tracking informal learning experiences

- Maintaining a detailed record of an individual's learning experiences

- Sophisticated reporting tools that can pull data from any LRS

- Letting the learner own his data and then decide whom to share that data[3]

In short, if you know what technologies you need to do training well, and you know how to pick the right technologies, the road ahead is very exciting!

Next up, Jon will explain how to take Flipped Learning outside of the context of training to flip meetings.

Chapter 9

Not Just Flipped Training, Flipped Meetings

It is estimated that $37 billion is wasted on unnecessary meetings every year. Middle managers spend an average of 35% of their time in meetings, while upper management spends 50%.[1]

Years ago, I was on the staff of a school that had painful faculty meetings. The meetings were poorly planned and were simply a dissemination of information. Often, decisions—in which the staff had little say—had already been made. As in many organizations, the meeting leaders rarely asked for feedback. During one meeting a colleague and I noticed a couple of staff members making tick marks on paper, looking at their watches, and smiling at each other. Afterward, we approached them and asked them what they were doing. They explained that at the beginning of the year they had "drafted" different faculty members into their

"Fantasy Faculty Meetings Competition." When somebody spoke, the person who had "drafted" that player received a point. And if the person talked for longer than a prescribed number of minutes, they got bonus points. As you can imagine, there were some people who always feel the need to talk during a meeting. These people were the top draft picks in the game.

This story has a point. What inspired these people to invent this game? They didn't see the purpose of the meetings. Nor did they feel like their input was important, and they realized that the meetings were a complete waste of time. You don't want to be that meeting leader.

Another illustration of ineffective meetings will illustrate some of the problems with ineffective meetings, but this one had fatal consequences. In a recent conversation with David Sternela, Training and Program Manager at AbbVie Pharmaceutical, he and I talked about how too many corporate meetings turn into painful PowerPoint presentations. Sternela told me about how a bad PowerPoint presentation had disastrous consequences with NASA's Space Shuttle Columbia.

If you recall, approximately 82 seconds after liftoff, NASA had images of a small piece of foam that broke off the fuel tank and struck the left wing, harming its thermal protection. Engineers on the ground analyzed the images, talked with the astronauts, and had many meetings with key scientists to ascertain the threat that the incident posed for the mission. Three reports were written and then converted into PowerPoint slides. The PowerPoint slides used a hierarchical structure with bullet points, sub-bullet points, and sub-sub bullet points. It was later concluded that using PowerPoint as an information delivery structure minimized important safety considerations which ended in disaster. One of the key findings was: "Serious problems require a serious tool: written reports. For nearly all engineering and scientific communication, instead of PowerPoint, the presentation and reporting software should be a word-processing program capable of capturing, editing, and publishing text, tables, data graphics, images, and scientific notation."[2] In other words, the biggest danger—the risk of an explosion—was minimized by the way it appeared in PowerPoint, and, tragically, lives were lost.

As I reflected on this, I thought back to my years as a teacher. I remember how excited I was when PowerPoint was introduced. I first started using it in the 1990s, fully expecting it to revolutionize my teaching, help students get higher test scores, and make concepts clearer and easier to understand. It comes as no surprise to you that this did not occur, and students still struggled with basic concepts and material regardless of how well I presented the content. The problem was that my classes were essentially the same. I stood at the center of the classroom parsing out information to students. This led to a passive classroom regardless of the nature of the presentation.

Meetings, too, can be a passive exercise in which participants see very little use in the information. They have little buy-in, their opinions are not taken into consideration, and the meetings feel like a giant waste of time. What if you flipped a meeting? What if meeting time was reclaimed rather than wasted? What if the same question we asked with Flipped Training was applied to meetings: What is the best use of your face-to-face (meeting) time?

The Flipped Learning model does not just apply to training settings. Meetings can also be flipped. Imagine a corporate meeting where participants are engaged, interested, and on task. Some time ago I challenged Paul Hermes, an associate principal in Wisconsin, to flip his staff meetings. He took me up on the challenge and flipped his meetings, and that in turn completely transformed the school climate. He shared that once he flipped his staff meetings, he netted twenty-four hours of training time for his teachers. The same question about the best use of face-to-face training time applies to flipped meetings. What is the best use of meeting time? We argue that the answer is not the introduction of new material or "death by PowerPoint."

How do you flip a meeting? How do we get away from death by PowerPoint?

IT STARTS WITH A PLAN

Too many meetings are a waste of time because the meeting organizer has failed to plan an effective meeting. And planning a flipped meeting is more work than planning a standard meeting. You can't just slap together an agenda, hand it out as participants walk in the room, and expect the best. Some might argue that the extra time is too much of a burden on the meeting leader. But when you consider how much time and resources a company ties up in meetings, making them tight, and efficient is a no-brainer. When planning a flipped meeting, the organizer needs to both develop the pre-work and create an environment in which meeting participants can deeply engage in the topic at hand. We wonder if one of the reasons flipped meetings are so effective is because meeting leaders must actually plan them.

A flipped meeting consists of the same two parts as a Flipped Training: the Individual Space and the Group Space. The only big difference is that the Group Space is not a training session, but rather a meeting. Let's dissect each of these and offer some suggestions to maximize both the Individual Space and the Group Space in the context of flipped meetings.

INDIVIDUAL SPACE PLANNING

Should you expect meeting participants to come to a meeting having completed the Individual Space work? Since every meeting has different objectives and each company culture is different, we will look at a variety of options that you can pick and choose from. We understand that corporate professionals are very busy, and expecting them to pre-watch a video or to read a document might not work for every meeting. Some options are:

- Hold them accountable: If meeting participants must do pre-work, then hold them accountable. Use software tools which monitor video viewership. If participants do not do the pre-work, call them out. These tools tell you who watched a video, how long she watched a video, and some allow for interspersing questions throughout the video.

- Start as if they all did the work: Begin the meeting with the assumption that everybody has done the pre-work and start from there. This communicates that this is the expectation of all participants. Participants who have not completed the pre-work will feel left out.

- Build the pre-work into the meeting itself. Start the meeting with a quiet time where participants engage with the Individual Space work alone. If you choose a flipped video, make sure meeting participants watch individually. This is critical because the goal is for participants to pause, rewind, and take notes, so that when the conversation starts they are ready to engage. The meeting leader may need to provide headphones to facilitate individual interaction. If you choose to flip using some text, simply having some quiet time around a conference room table is sufficient. Jeff Bezos has adopted this practice at Amazon, where the first fifteen minutes of a meeting is devoted to "study hall" where meeting participants go over a 4-6 page narrative document written by the meeting leader. After fifteen minutes the meeting begins.[3]

Make sure that the content of either the video or the reading directly applies to the meeting. If you require participants to do pre-work, create high-quality, engaging, and relevant material. Make sure everybody at the meeting knows this will be a flipped meeting so that they are prepared to be an active participant.

GROUP SPACE PLANNING

Like an effective Flipped Training session, the "magic" of a flipped meeting happens in the Group Space. The Group Space is where the most amount of thought and energy must be directed. Make the meeting so awesome that people walk out and say, "Now that was a valuable meeting." Get creative: actually make a decision, debate, ideate, or go deep. Use some of the ideas from the Group Space chapter (Chapter 7) to come up with creative uses of the meeting time. Below are a few suggestions which might invigorate your meetings.

- Spend some time listening and getting feedback on the pre-work.

- Ask for better ideas or solutions to pressing problems.

- Build in an activity which will deepen discussion, like a case study, customer story, or simulation.

Above all, don't waste people's time. They need to see the both the value of the meeting and their value in the meeting. If you don't have both of these elements, you probably should not have the meeting.

BEST PRACTICES FOR AN EFFECTIVE FLIPPED MEETING

Overall, there are some principles which must be incorporated into any meeting, flipped or not. But with flipped meetings, the importance of these principles is often amplified. We encourage you to heed these suggestions to maximize your meeting times.

- Have a clear purpose for the meeting. Always ask: What is the reason for this meeting? If there is none, you should cancel.

- Tie the pre-work to the meeting action items.

- Make sure everyone at the meeting should be at the meeting. If they don't need to be there, excuse them.

- Make sure everyone at the meeting has a voice in any decisions made. There is nothing more frustrating than being in a meeting where the

decisions have been made, and your input is not
valued.

- Start and end on time.

- Leave participants with action items for them to do
  before the next meeting.

- Involve everyone in the meeting.

- Learn how to facilitate a discussion. Meeting
  leaders may need to hone their skills and learn how
  to facilitate a discussion, which is a different skill
  than sharing information.

- Meeting leaders often suffer from diarrhea of the
  mouth. Don't dominate the meeting.

- Listen! Most companies hire smart people. Listen to
  employees.

- Rein in the dominant participants. You know
  who they are. Be prepared to gently move the
  discussion on when a few people dominate.

- Ask the quiet for their input. Often the introverts
  have the best suggestions.

- Acknowledge people. Take some time to ask about
  their families, and take an interest in the lives of
  the people in your organization. Showing that
  you genuinely care goes a long way to creating
  a positive meeting culture. You may not want to
  spend a huge amount of time on this, but simple
  acknowledgments will transform your culture.

- Debrief: Ask the question: How could we have done better with this meeting?

There is no one way to run an effective flipped meeting. Though there are principles to follow, each meeting leader needs to customize and choose the best techniques that work for your context and your personality. Have fun and have the humility to learn from mistakes and missteps.

IT'S ABOUT CULTURE CHANGE

We talked with one organization that worked hard to flip their meetings but struggled. The meeting leader spent a great deal of time creating a document for each meeting participant to read ahead of time, and everybody read it. But he struggled when it came to the group meeting space. The meeting was well designed, and he had organized some great conversations and input mechanisms.

However, a small group dominated the meeting time, and, pushing their agenda, took over the meeting. The trainer wanted to step in, but since the few who dominated the meeting included the CEO, he felt powerless to change the tone. After the meeting, those whose voices had not been heard came to the meeting organizer and said, "There was nothing you could have done. They dominate all our meetings." To successfully flip a meeting, egos must be checked at the door, and those in attendance should understand that everyone will have an impact on any decision that might be made. This leads us to the last issue in flipping a meeting: how to build a meeting culture that values everybody's input and maximizes meeting time.

Change is hard, and changing the culture at a company is probably one of the hardest things to accomplish. Though flipping a meeting sounds like a great idea, it will take determination and grit to change the culture. But change must start somewhere. We believe you will be pleasantly surprised to see productivity increasing, higher levels of engagement, and more efficient meetings in which time is not wasted.

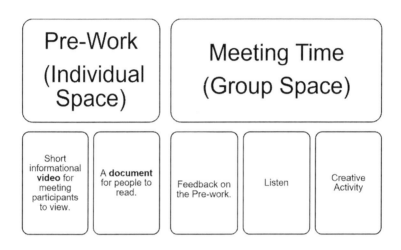

Figure 9.1: Summary of a Flipped Meeting

Now it is your turn. It all starts with an intentional plan before the process of cultural change can begin. Transform your corporate culture one meeting at a time.

Next up I will continue the discussion by guiding organizations, trainers, and trainees through the culture change necessary to implement Flipped Learning.

Chapter 10

Creating a Flipped Culture

"This is the way we've always done it." These eight words are the death of too many change initiatives. Changing the mindset of trainers, staff, managers, and upper management is critical. This axiom is especially true when we talk about Flipped Learning since it represents a seismic shift away from traditional training. Trainers must get comfortable with getting away from the front of the room. Frankly, this was hard for me. I loved being the center of attention in my classrooms for nineteen years. I was good at delivering information and, at least in my opinion; I was a true expert. But when I decided to flip my class, I had to give it up. And I can say categorically; it was the BEST thing I ever did in education. The beauty was that I was still able to present information, but instead of doing it live in front of a group of students, I did it on a micro-video. I have worked with thousands of teachers and trainers around the world, and this mindset change is by far the most difficult hurdle to overcome. Ultimately, trainers must dispel the notion that they must be the fount of all knowledge and the deliverer of everything. In this chapter, we will explore some practical ways to help your organization become a place where Flipped Learning is not the exception, but rather the norm.

BUY- IN FROM THE TOP

Tom Phelps, the Training and Development Specialist at Fisch and Richardson, an intellectual properties legal firm, shared how critical it was for him to get leaders onboard. Since senior management sets the tone for an organization, when they get behind Flipped Learning, the likelihood of its success increases exponentially. Early on, Phelps realized he needed to get buy-in for this change from every aspect of his organization. Before he implemented Flipped Learning, he took the time to make a case for change before senior management. I wasn't privy to the meeting, but he shared that in his pitch he had three main points: the cost of training would decrease (all senior leaders love that!), proficiency would increase, and the firm's bottom line would be positively impacted.

In his case, it was an easy sell because there is great pressure on law firms to have employees proficient in the use of technology. In fact, inefficient technology users are often let go. As you may know, law firms typically charge per hour for their services, so it would seem counterintuitive to have efficient employees. However, in 2015, Casey Flaherty, who was in-house counsel for Kia Motors, surmised that Kia was paying its outside counsel too much money for technical inefficiency. He devised a "Legal Tech Audit," which tested outside counsel's efficient use of simple tools such as Microsoft Word and Excel. The eight firms he tested all failed. Kia did not want to pay for work that represented an inefficient use of technology.[1] This set off a paradigm shift in legal circles, and now firms like Day Pitney need to make sure their employees are technologically savvy. These days, many companies are asking law firms to take the Legal Tech Audit before they hire them. Thus, if an employee takes two hours to do a task that should take only one hour, a firm may lose a client. This has accelerated the need for quality technology training of legal firms. If an employee is not performing, the employee will be either re-trained or looking for another line of work.

We have met Crystal Fernandes-Harris and Carrie Kirby from the Day Pitney law firm in New York several times. They too felt the need to get buy-in from the top. At their firm, learning has always been a high priority. The thing they had to sell was the flipped nature of the training, which they were able to do. And as they implemented it, the results were astounding. They recently won the Academy of Human Resource Development's 2017 Excellence in Scholarly Practice Award for their innovative program.

Getting buy-in from leadership is crucial. Now, we realize that many of you may not have access to your CEO, and many CEOs are not aware of what happens in the training department, but to the degree you can at least inform senior staff, that will be huge. One way to get buy-in would be to teach senior management how to flip meetings. After all, meetings are probably one of their biggest pain points.

BUY- IN FROM TRAINERS

By now, we are familiar with Cathy Mongeau. She is head of the sales training divisions of AbbVie Pharmaceutical. Trainers come from the sales force and work for eighteen months at a time before they either go back to the sales ranks or possibly move onto a sales manager role. She shares with new trainers that they will be flipping the training, and the expectation is that trainers are on-board.

But what if you don't have the luxury of trainers who must buy in? Don't worry, we have some strategies. One of the greatest things about Flipped Learning in the world of "schooling" is that it didn't start out in an ivory tower or at the superintendent's office. It started in rooms 313 and 314 at a small rural school in Colorado. We didn't ask our principal or our superintendent; we simply changed the way we had always taught. It was a grass-roots movement started by teachers to reach students. This bottom-up approach is also happening in the corporate space. A few corporate trainers have seen the future and have stepped out to change the way training is done.

The bigger issue I found when chatting with these trailblazers is that many of them struggled to bring other trainers in their organization onboard. They were trailblazing while others were dragging their feet. This is analogous to the K-12 world where only a few teachers flip their classes, and the rest are stuck in a 19th-century educational model. How do you get buy-in from your whole training staff?

As stated earlier, changing someone's mindset is very hard. Let me offer a few suggestions:

- Pick the right trainers. Every organization has early adopters—people ready to make the leap. Identify these people and start with them. In the beginning, you can ignore those who you know are reluctant to change.

188

- Start small with a pilot group. Start with one training course taught by a group of people who are the "right trainers." Pick training that has low impact, so you can learn the ropes about how to best implement Flipped Learning in your context.

- Support innovative trainers. If you have trainers stepping outside the box, support them and give them the resources to succeed.

- Share your success. Once you have learned from your pilot group, begin to share the successes. Talk about it at the water cooler, and share the results with senior management, in newsletters, and at staff meetings.

- Collect data. There is nothing more powerful than cold, hard facts. Did your trainees score higher on a certification exam? Did the training cost less money? Did the training lead to greater efficiency at your call center? Did the training obtain rave reviews from trainees?

The best way to spread Flipped Learning has always been to go out and do the best you can at flipping a single course. When done well, Flipped Learning simply works! And as you flip well, other trainers will notice, employees will talk it up, the CEO will notice, and after a time, Flipped Learning can spread throughout your organization.

BUY - IN FROM TRAINEES

Trainees also need to be brought up to speed on Flipped Learning. They are most likely used to learning passively. As we discussed in the chapter on Best Practices (Chapter 5), it is vital that you teach trainees how to learn in a Flipped

Learning environment. Usually, this is not too difficult, since Flipped Learning makes sense, is easy to understand, and, when effectively implemented, sells itself. But if getting trainees on board is a struggle, then I recommend that you take some time at the beginning of the program to communicate the reasons for flipping your training. I have found that the three images of Bloom's Taxonomy (from Chapter 1) are the most powerful images you can share when explaining Flipped Learning. All trainees understand that the point of their job is to do their job, which typically means the application and analysis levels of Bloom's Taxonomy. Your training time will be maximized to the extent that you can focus the training time on application and analysis.

MARKETING YOUR TRAINING

As business people, you know that marketing—of a product, service, or idea—is everything. And marketing Flipped Learning to trainees, trainers, staff, and management is no different. The beauty is that Flipped Learning is an easy sell. When it is well explained and well implemented, people clamor for it. I had the privilege of working with Warren Township High School in Gurnee, Illinois, where five teachers were early adopters. When they first started flipping their classes, students were asking to leave. They weren't too sure about this crazy idea where the teachers weren't "teaching anymore." But as the year progressed, those students who stayed in the flipped classes began to really dig it. They shared their enthusiasm with their peers, and by the second semester, students were transferring in. Other teachers started to notice and asked the flipped teachers what they were doing. Today, more than 75 teachers are flipping in that school, and students are now asking their non-flipped teachers why they haven't flipped.

How can you make what happened at Warren Township occur in your organization? Below are a few suggestions:

- Meetings: During staff meetings, try to get four minutes to share about the new training paradigm.

- Send out short emails explaining Flipped Learning.

- Send out short video training to employees. I did this with my staff and called my videos Tech-Tip Tuesdays. This gave them a feel for a flipped environment and then when I had them in a training room, we were able to apply, analyze, and go deeper.

- Flip a meeting (see Chapter 9) so people get a feel for a Flipped Learning environment.

- Be a relentless advocate for Flipped Learning. Sometimes the squeaky wheel gets the oil. At some point, people will start to take notice.

- Share how Flipped Learning will save time.

- Share how Flipped Learning will increase learning retention.

- Share Flipped Learning studies.

- Find creative ways to communicate. Tom Phelps of Fish and Richardson had little success getting employees to come to voluntary Flipped Training until he started sending out calendar invites instead of emails.

Lastly, remember that Flipped Learning is, as Wayne Gretzky said, "where the puck is going to be." Flipped Learning is a way to set your company apart from your competition. Clients likely will be intrigued that you have flipped, and this discriminator might just help you win that next contract or promotion.

THINK LONG-TERM

Creating a Flipped Learning culture will not happen overnight. It takes time and commitment. Chart out a one- to three-year plan. In the first cycle (a year, a quarter, or a training cycle), choose one course to flip and learn from it. You will want to figure out what technology you will need in the Individual Space and how to best use the Group Space. In the second cycle, add one more course and continue to iterate and customize. Also during the second cycle, bring in more trainers and teach them how to flip their courses effectively. Then, repeat the process as you see the need until you have flipped the training at your organization. I have enjoyed working with corporations on both their long-term and short-term plans. Sitting down with trainers and helping them design their courses has opened my eyes to the potential and promise of Flipped Learning in Corporate Training.

Timing matters! Make sure you don't initiate change concurrently with a new product rollout or at a particularly busy time of the year for your organization. Graph out a year, putting all the change initiatives, busy times, and other critical happenings at your organization on the x-axis with the amount of time/change required on the y-axis. Find a place where flux is at a minimum and try implementing Flipped Learning during that time.

And don't give up! Flipped Learning works. But if you give up too early in the cycle, you will miss out on one of the best things in all of training. You may potentially miss out on deep learning, lasting change, and impact that will propel your organization to new heights.

Next up, Errol will tie the whole book together as he looks to the future of Flipped Learning in training.

Chapter 11

Visionaries, Thought Leaders & the Future of Training

As you know, there are a lot of very bright people out there thinking about L&D. We were deeply inspired by the work of several thought leaders who are rethinking what training is and what training can be. Standing on their shoulders, we were able to see more clearly what's possible with Flipped Learning in corporate training and how to get from here to there.

With that, let's walk out to the leading edge of corporate training and peer into the minds of these innovative thinkers.

THOUGHT LEADERS

Clark Quinn, Ph.D., is the executive director of Quinnovation and has been helping organizations deliver strategic learning technology solutions for more than three decades. Clark combines a deep background in the learning sciences with broad experience in technology applications, which he applies to corporate, government, education, and nonprofit sectors. He's the author of *Engaging Learning: Designing e-Learning Simulation Games; Designing mLearning: Tapping into the Mobile Revolution for Organizational Performance*; and *The Mobile Academy: mLearning for Higher Education.*

Big Idea: Rethinking technology use in training and performance support.

- "Our industry isn't using technology in ways that align with how people really think, work, and learn. But it can—and should . . . A large part of the L&D Revolution will require practitioners to flip the way we employ technology."

- "Trying to get people to remember details about every product offering or trouble shooting procedures is an exercise in futility. Let's face it: it is hard to get knowledge in the head. Therefore, I propose that for the first flip we should be using technology to present information at the time of need—not trying to get it in the head every worker before they need to use it."

- "Second, performers are good at making decisions when they are well supported. So we should match the task to the tool, and have the tools hold the rote information and support performers through the decision process."[1]

David Grebow is CEO at KnowledgeStar. He was a founding Executive Core Team member of the IBM Institute for Advanced Learning, where his research focused on collaborative learning environments. Grebow is a contributor to Creating a Learning Culture and author of *A Compass for the Knowledge Economy Business: How-to Succeed in the New Knowledge Economy*, and he served on the Editorial Review Board for Information Age Publishing. Grebow is also currently launching an app-based Interactive Performance Support System™ to provide operational, compliance and safety information to people working in manufacturing and industrial environments as part of his Internet of Smart Things™ program.

Big Idea: Moving from "push" training to a "pull" learning model.

- "The highest-performing corporations are abandoning traditional 'push' training for the 'pull' learning model. Push training is a centralized, top-down model that occurs when management determines what it is people need to know or do and 'push' educational programs out from a central training group. Going to a class or taking an assigned online program is push training."

- "'Pull learning' is the model for the new Knowledge Economy. It is a decentralized, bottom-up approach that enables employees to access the information they need when it is needed. . . . Replacing push training with pull learning transforms an organization into a learning culture."[2]

- "I have seen the future of on-the-job learning. It is an app that connects any piece of machinery your company uses, with any Internet-connected device you already have, and instantly and automatically delivers any specifically chosen, task-related information that exists in the cloud . . . your device provides information that can range from details about how it works, technical support information, or even safety checklists to ensure compliance. You decide."[3]

Stephen J. Gill is principal of Stephen J. Gill Consulting. His expertise is in creating learning cultures in organizations and measuring the impact of learning and performance improvement interventions. He has done this work for more than 25 years, since leaving the faculty of the University of Michigan's School of Education. He has written extensively on these topics. His most recent books are *Getting More From Your Investment in Training*: The 5As Framework, Developing a Learning Culture in Nonprofit Organizations, and Communication in High-Performance Organizations: Principles and Best Practices. Gill also posts regularly on The Performance Improvement Blog. He serves his community as an elected trustee of Washtenaw Community College.

Big Ideas: Creating a learning culture and self-directed learners.

- "In a training culture, responsibility for employee learning resides with instructors and training managers. In that kind of culture, the assumption is that trainers, under the direction of a chief learning officer (CLO), drive learning. In contrast, in a learning culture, responsibility for learning resides with employees, managers, and teams. In that kind of culture, employees are expected to seek knowledge and skills and apply that learning when and where it is needed."[4]

- "In the new knowledge economy, the pace of change is such that the push model of training can't keep up with organizational needs and with the way employees learn best. . . . Now companies need self-directed learners who can 'pull' the knowledge and skills required for their jobs, when and where they need it."[5]

- "We no longer have the luxury of time to define, design, develop, deliver, manage, and measure formal courses. Survival will require people who can... find their own curriculum and courses, figure out an appropriate way to learn, and get on with it. It's cliché to say it, but employees will have to learn how to learn in this new environment. And management will need to support self-learning, not direct it."[6]

Arun Pradhan is a senior learning and performance strategist for DeakinCo., one of Australia's leading providers of blended learning and performance solutions, and is the creator of the Learn2Learn app. With nearly two decades of experience, he has taken the lead creative role in delivering learning campaigns and performance ecosystems to some of Australia's largest banks, telcos, and retailers. Pradhan is passionate about leveraging the latest developments in neuroscience, evidence-based learning, and technology to create positive and lasting change for people and organizations.

Big Idea: Reconnecting learning and work.

- "From our youth, schools told us that we learn about the world in a classroom, rather than presenting the world as our classroom. It's no wonder that a culture of continuous learning can sometimes feel elusive as a result."[7]

- "How and why can L&D embrace the fact that we learn from work? What can be done to burst the 'training bubble' where formal learning is delivered as an event, separate to the workflow?"[8]

- "Companies wanting to overcome the training blight and become learning organizations have an urgent need for a more holistic approach, of which formal training plays an important role to help introduce ideas, prime mindset, and develop conceptual frameworks, but it's just one element of a broader on the job and social experience."[9]

Charles Jennings is a member of the Internet Time Alliance and co-founder of the 70:20:10 Institute. (The 70:20:10 model states that employees get 70 percent of their knowledge from on-the-job tasks, 20 percent from developmental relationships, and 10 percent from formal training.) Jennings is a leading thinker and practitioner in learning, development, and performance in the United Kingdom.

Big Idea: Solving the learning transfer problem.

- "There can be no challenge to the fact that a major problem exists with learning transfer, and that it's existed for years. It could be argued that it came into existence the day we separated training from the workplace. . . . One of the best ways to overcome the learning or training 'transfer' problem can be simply to eliminate the need for it."

- "The way we learn best is when the stimuli are relevant to our need. Learning is a highly contextual activity. The closer to the point of use that it occurs the more effective it is likely to be."

- "If learning is embedded in the daily flow of work, rather than away from the workflow, the idea that we need to develop ways to 'transfer' that learning into practical use disappears. When there's little or no gap between the two, there is no 'transfer problem.' When we learn from work (rather than learning to work), even better."[10]

Bob Mosher is a senior partner and chief learning evangelist for APPLY Synergies, a strategic consulting firm.

Big Ideas: Compliance and performance support

- "For the most part, we've created an event-based solution for a workflow/performance problem. Compliance is not measured at a point in time; it's demonstrated throughout the lifetime of employment. Yes, it's important to get up to speed on knowledge, to demonstrate a certain level of understanding around compliance issues, but performing in a compliant way happens in the workflow; that's where our solutions need to target."

- "We need to take a closer look at the tools and methodologies emerging in workflow learning such as performance support and adaptive learning. These tools are not designed as training solutions, but rather as ways to guide, support and reassess employees at the appropriate moment of performance need, as they navigate the workflow. "

- "Adaptive learning is a technology-based approach that . . . pushes relevant learning to the individual when it is needed. When this approach is married with training and performance support, the overall solution offers measurable support well beyond an event-based strategy. . . . This isn't a pipe dream. There are organizations doing this right now, and they are being recognized for it."[11]

Dr. Conrad Gottfredson is the co-author of Innovative Performance Support: Tools and Strategies for Learning in the Workflow and a contributing author to Timothy Clark's book *The Employee Engagement Mindset: The Six Drivers for Tapping into the Hidden Potential of Everyone in Your Company.* He is also a regular author in many industry magazines such as CLO Magazine. He has developed and presented public seminars to many thousands of participants both nationally and internationally. Gottfredson formulated the 5 Moments of Learning Need framework and developed the AGILE model for Instructional design.

Big Idea: Rethinking when and where training is most relevant.

Gottfredson has proposed that there are five moments (listed below) when a learner needs information in order to do a job well. Each of these represents learning opportunities. The first two involve acquiring knowledge and are suited to traditional training systems. The last three involve applying knowledge and call for performance support systems.

1. When learning for the first time

2. When learning more

3. When remembering and/or applying what's been learned

4. When things go wrong

5. When things change[12]

Elliot Masie is an internationally recognized futurist, analyst, researcher and organizer on the critical topics of workforce learning, business collaboration and emerging technologies. He is the editor of Learning TRENDS by Elliott Masie, an Internet newsletter read by over 52,000 business executives worldwide, and a regular columnist for professional publications, including CLO Magazine. He is the author of a dozen books and is the convener of Learning 2015 (Orlando, Florida) and Global Learning Forum (Dubai). He heads The MASIE Center, a Saratoga Springs, NY, think tank focused on how organizations can support learning and knowledge within the workforce. He leads the Learning CONSORTIUM, a coalition of 230 global organizations cooperating on the evolution of learning strategies, including CNN, Wal-Mart, American Express, Farmers Insurance, Emirates Airline, Starbucks, General Electric and Fidelity Investments.

Big Idea: Optimizing on-the-job learning

- "Few, if any, organizations today can expect to keep up with the speed of change without effective on-the-job learning (OJL) practices."

- "People are most attuned to learning in the context of their work. They are much more ready to engage mentally, emotionally and physically in learning while they are in their workflow than they are when they step away from it to learn in the traditional or virtual classroom, or an eLearning course."

- "The actual nature of 21st-century learners is resistant to learning options that are delayed and removed from the here and now. Learners are predisposed to walk away from lengthy, structured learning solutions and look elsewhere for the shortest path to effective on-the-job performance."[13]

Bottom-Line Performance publishes the Learning and Remembering Survey. According to 2017 survey results, respondents were most excited about one learning trend in particular: Microlearning.

Big Ideas: Solving the learning loss problem with Microlearning.

- "Microlearning can take many different shapes. Some use short videos. Others create short tutorials that are mobile-optimized. Many turn to bite-sized games. . . . Microlearning . . . is like a batch of mini-muffins: easy to eat in just a few bites. . . . It allows learners to focus on a single objective for about 5-7 minutes at a time."

- "Microlearning is a valuable reinforcement method. . . . What do you really think sales reps will remember from a 3-day product launch meeting if you don't follow up after training? Microlearning allows you to reinforce the most important concepts and need-to-know information after a training event without requiring a large time commitment from learners."

- "Busy employees need something quick and easy to access. . . Most people simply don't have time to take training all at once. But Microlearning could be a good solution to help people fit learning into their busy schedules."

- "Microlearning can't help learners go from novice to expert. When you need to help learners become experts, a Microlearning module is not enough. It takes longer periods of time to develop more in-depth knowledge or advanced skills."[14]

These thought leaders reveal an exciting picture of what's happening on the leading edge of L&D. They also cast a riveting vision for the future of training and learning in this brave new world. They leave our minds blown, after exploding with thoughts about adaptive learning, JITT, mobile learning, gamification, killer learning apps, Microlearning, improving learning transfer, ending learning loss, overhauling compliance training, and creating "pull learning" cultures that enable us to develop talent at the speed required for businesses to succeed in the 21st Century.

This is heady stuff.

But then it happens. We come down from the adrenaline-fueled high of considering the myriad possibilities, and corrosive thoughts begin to overcome us: "Okay, I get it, these are all of the amazing new things we can do in corporate training, but how do we do them?" Simply said, how do we get from here to there?

THE OPERATING SYSTEM FOR THE
FUTURE OF L&D

Somewhere along this book-writing journey, we saw clearly that Flipped Learning has a role to play in the future of corporate training. First, we noticed the obvious applications where Flipped Learning could naturally fit. Then we began to see the specialized corporate training problems that Flipped Learning is uniquely equipped to solve. By the time we got to the leading edge of corporate training, we had another awakening:

Flipped Learning is the pivotal missing link in the future of learning and development.

Wait! Before you unfriend me, unfollow us, or write a blistering critique on Twitter, consider the three key problems Flipped Learning solves.

1. Meeting your staff where they are. It's safe to say that the overwhelming masses of people you are responsible for training were educated in the traditional teacher-led, sit-and-get, "push" learning model. People who were not trained to "own their learning," "be self-directed" learners, or "pull" the knowledge they need when they need it are going to require a bridge to the future of learning and development. That bridge is Flipped Learning 3.0. In short, "learning to learn" is baked into the Flipped Learning model.

2. A proven change model. Moving decision makers, trainers, and trainees toward the future of learning is easy to write about, but much harder to do. Flipped Learning 3.0 is a proven system for moving people from

the past into the future of learning. In learning scenarios all around the world, Flipped Learning has transported trainers and trainees into the future in manageable baby steps. The migration process is adaptable enough to manage different learning styles, skill sets, learning populations, generations, cultures, languages, special needs, diverse processing speeds, growth mindsets, and training budgets.

3. Flipped Learning is pluralistic. As we discussed in Chapter 3, it doesn't matter what training principle you've fallen in love with, what technology you're excited about, or what instructional model you're using; Flipped Learning can support and enhance your current system. Whether your current training is primarily instructor-led or almost completely delivered online, Flipped Learning 3.0 can make it more effective and move your model toward the future of learning and development.

Beyond these three basic benefits, Flipped Learning:

- Creates the time and the structure for optimal learning;

- Provides a proven guide to creating effective micro content;

- Clarifies the best use of class time;

- Has a successful track record of getting trainees to embrace owning their learning;

- Provides a coherent blueprint for explaining the instructional model to stakeholders;

- Acknowledges the social nature of optimal learning that can't be digitized;

- And offers a guide for planning how to "time-shift and "location-shift" training based on the "five moments of need."

These are the inflection points that L&D professionals are grappling with as they look to the future of corporate training and learning. As for CEOs? The late Jay Cross said it best: "Executives don't want learning; they want execution."[15]

Understanding how to think about the expanding array of emerging training trends, tools, platforms, technologies, and apps can be daunting. But if we've done our job, it should be clear that Flipped Learning is not just another instructional model like gamification, adaptive learning, mobile learning, or Microlearning. Flipped Learning is a framework that allows you to plan, choose, deploy, manage, and support any of these other applications.

Flipped Learning's ability to support and enhance all other instructional "apps" is why we call Flipped Learning the operating system for the future of corporate training and learning.

TAKING THE FIRST STEP

Many still look at Flipped Learning as that concept they've heard about already. This perspective prevents some from grasping what Flipped Learning 3.0 has become and how it is the bridge to the future of corporate training.

As mentioned in the preface, Flipped Learning is a lot like the famous optical illusion called "the young lady and the old hag." Look at it one way, and you see an old woman. Look at it in a slightly different way, and you see a beautiful maiden brimming with future possibilities.

The most important step you can take toward the future of corporate training is to simply adjust your perspective. Play with the notion of Flipped Learning as the operating system for the future of corporate training and watch what happens. We think you'll be pleasantly surprised.

We close with a thought from Arie de Geus, the former head of Shell Oil Company's Strategic Planning Group:

"The ability to learn faster than your competitors may be the only sustainable competitive advantage."

If we combine the wisdom of Toffler we shared at the opening, with de Geus we get a powerful perspective that prepares us for the future.

*The ability to learn, **unlearn** and **relearn** faster than your competitors may be the only sustainable competitive advantage.*

We've turned off the "fasten your seat belts" sign. You are now free to move about—and, ideally, away from the front of the classroom!

ENDNOTES

Chapter 1

1.   Johnson, L., Adams Becker, S., Estrada, V., and Freeman, A. (2015). NMC Horizon Report: 2015 Higher Education Edition. Austin, Texas: The New Media Consortium.

2.   Definition of Flipped Learning. (2014, March 12). Retrieved from http://flippedlearning.org/definition-of-flipped-learning/

3.   Cross, P. (2005). What do we know about students' learning and how do we know it? *University of California, Berkeley, Center for Studies in Higher Education,* 7.05. Retrieved from www.cshe.berkeley.edu/sites/default/files/shared/publications/docs/ROP.Cross.7.05.pdf

4.   Chickering, A. W., &Gamson, Z. F. (1987). Seven principles for good practice in undergraduate education. *The Wingspread Journal,9*(2).

5.   Bloom, B., Englehart, M. Furst, E., Hill, W., &Krathwohl, D. (1956). *Taxonomy of educational objectives: The classification of educational goals. Handbook I: Cognitive domain.* New York, Toronto: Longmans, Green.

6.   Anderson, L.W., &Krathwohl, D.R. (2001). *A taxonomy for learning, teaching, and assessing: A revision of Bloom's Taxonomy of educational objectives.* New York: Longman.

Chapter 2

1.   Benton, D. A. (1999). *How to think like a CEO: The 22 vital traits you need to be the person at the top.* New York: Warner Books.

2.   (2016). 2016 Training Industry Report. *Training,* 28-41. Retrieved from https://trainingmag.com/sites/default/files/images/Training_Industry_Report_2016.pdf

3.   Great Place to Work Institute. (2014). *Guide to greatness.* San Francisco, CA: Great Place to Work.

4.   Rothwell, W. J. (2003). *What CEOs expect from corporate training: Building workplace learning and performance initiatives that advance organization goals.* New York: AMACOM.

5.   Buss, C. (2006, February 14). *How CEOs think.* Retrieved from https://www.td.org/Publications/Newsletters/Links/2006/02/How-Ceos-Think

6.   Ibid.

7.   Bersin by Deloitte. (2009). *2009 corporate learning factbook reveals 11% decline in corporate training spending* [Press release]. Retrieved from https://www.bersin.com/News/Content.aspx?id=8438

8.   Bullen, D. (2014, December 1). *How top companies make the ROI case for employee training.* Retrieved from http://www.skilledup.com/insights/how-top-companies-make-the-roi-case-for-employee-training

9.   Ibid.

10.   Wentworth, D. (2016, November 30). *Top spending trends for training, 2016-2017.* Retrieved from https://trainingmag.com/top-spending-trends-training-2016-2017

11.   DeSmet, A., McGurk, M., & Schwartz, E. (2010, October). Getting more from your training programs. *McKinsey Quarterly.* Retrieved from http://www.mckinsey.com/business-functions/organization/our-insights/getting-more-from-your-training-programs

12.   Gill, S. J. (2015, November 24). Industry report: Too much training; not enough learning [Blog post]. Retrieved from http://stephenjgill.typepad.com/performance_improvement_b/2015/11/industry-report-too-much-training-not-enough-learning.html

13.   Hermann Ebbinghaus. (n.d.). In *Encyclopaedia Britannica online.* Retrieved from https://www.britannica.com/biography/Hermann-Ebbinghaus

14.   (2016). 2016 Training Industry Report. *Training,* 28-41. Retrieved from https://trainingmag.com/sites/default/files/images/Training_Industry_Report_2016.pdf

15.   Banna, S. (2014, September 8). *Face-to-face training is still the better choice over digital lessons.* Retrieved from https://www.td.org/Publications/Magazines/TD/TD-Archive/2014/09/Webex-Face-to-Face-Training-Is-Still-the-Better-Choice

16.   Bullen, D. (2014, December 1). *How top companies make the ROI case for employee training.* Retrieved from http://www.skilledup.com/insights/how-top-companies-make-the-roi-case-for-employee-training

17.   Aronson, N. &Arfstrom, K. M. (2013). Flipped learning in higher education. Retrieved from http://www. flippedlearning.org/cms/lib07/VA01923112/Centricity/ Domain/41/HigherEdWhitePaper%20FINAL.pdf

Chapter 3

1.   Boller, S. (2017, January 10). *Seven 2017 learning trends: Novel or norm?* Retrieved from http://www. bottomlineperformance.com/seven-2017-learning-trends-novel-or-norm/

2.   Yarbro, J., Arfstrom, K. M., McKnight, K., & McKnight, P. (2014). *Extension of a review of Flipped Learning.* Retrieved from http://flippedlearning.org/wp-content/uploads/2016/07/Extension-of-FLipped-Learning-Llt-Review-June-2014.pdf

3.   Technavio. (2016, May). *Global flip classroom market 2016-2020.* Chicago, IL.

Chapter 4

1.   Hilton, H. (2017, April 20). *6 pervasive corporate training pitfalls.* Retrieved from http://www. bottomlineperformance.com/6-pervasive-corporate-training-pitfalls/

2.   Giulioni, J. W. (2017, March 30). *Learning and development challenges in 2017.* Retrieved from https:// www.td.org/Publications/Blogs/Career-Development-Blog/2017/03/Learning-and-Development-Challenges-in-2017

3.   Student engagement more complex, changeable than thought. (2013, June 20). Retrieved from http://www.

news.pitt.edu/news/student-engagement-more-complex-changeable-thought

4.   Nielson, B. (2014, September 17). *How MOOCs can solve common training problems.* Retrieved from http://www.yourtrainingedge.com/how-moocs-can-solve-common-training-problems/

5.   Mosher, B. (2017, March 9). *Compliance training: Cheers or jeers?* Retrieved from http://www.clomedia.com/2017/03/09/compliance-training-cheers-jeers/

6.   The evidence indicating that flipped instruction works continues to grow. (n.d.). Retrieved from http://jackson.stark.k12.oh.us/webpages/bblackstock/index.cfm?subpage=1614797

7.   Smith, C. (2014, October 7). Spartan College sees results with curriculum overhaul. *Tulsa World.* Retrieved from http://www.tulsaworld.com/businesshomepage1/spartan-college-sees-results-with-curriculum-overhaul/article_63bb830b-4c4e-5a19-ac74-aaf722385311.html

8.   Bidwell, A. (2014, August 5). Flipped classroom may help weaker STEM students. *U.S. News & World Report.* Retrieved from https://www.usnews.com/news/stem-solutions/articles/2014/08/05/taking-a-page-from-humanities-college-engineering-gets-flipped

9.   Walsh, K. (2014, August 24). *Flipped learning pilot radically reduces DFW grade rates in two courses.* Retrieved from http://www.emergingedtech.com/2014/08/flipped-learning-pilot-reduces-dfw-grade-rates/

10.   An alternative vote. (2011, May 12). *The Economist.* Retrieved from http://www.economist.com/node/18678925

11.   DeSmet, A., McGurk, M., & Schwartz, E. (2010, October). Getting more from your training programs.

McKinsey Quarterly. Retrieved from http://www.mckinsey. com/business-functions/organization/our-insights/getting-more-from-your-training-programs

12.   Fitzpatrick, R. (2001, October). *The strange case of the transfer of training estimate.* Retrieved from http://www. siop.org/tip/backissues/TipOct01/03fitpatrick.aspx

13.   Saks, A. M., &Belcourt, M. (2006, November). An investigation of training activities and transfer of training in organizations. *Human Resource Management, 45*(4), 629-648. Retrieved from https://www.researchgate.net/ publication/227701783_An_investigation _of_training_activities_and_transfer_of_training_in_ organizations

14.   Gryger, L., Saar, T., &Schaar, P. (2010, March). *Building organizational capabilities: McKinsey Global Survey results.* Retrieved from http://www.mckinsey.com/business-functions/organization/our-insights/building-organizational-capabilities-mckinsey-global-survey-results

15.   Wentworth, D. (2016, November 30). *Top spending trends for training, 2016-2017.* Retrieved from https:// trainingmag.com/top-spending-trends-training-2016-2017

16.   Ibid.

17.   Gryger, L., Saar, T., &Schaar, P. (2010, March). *Building organizational capabilities: McKinsey Global Survey results.* Retrieved from http://www.mckinsey.com/business-functions/organization/our-insights/building-organizational-capabilities-mckinsey-global-survey-results

18.   Grebow, D. [David Grebow]. (n.d.). David Grebow [LinkedIn profile]. Retrieved from https://www.linkedin.com/ in/davidgrebow/

19. Grebow, D. (2013, April 9). The flipped corporate class? [Blog post]. Retrieved from https://knowledgestarblog. wordpress.com/2013/04/09/the-flipped-corporate-class/

20. Hilton, H. (2017, April 20). *6 pervasive corporate training pitfalls.* Retrieved from http://www. bottomlineperformance.com/6-pervasive-corporate-training-pitfalls/

21. Ulrich, Dave. "Emerging Trends in HR Value Creation." Greater Madison Area Society for Human Resource Management. Society for Human Resource Management, 22 Apr. 2016. Web., http://www.gmashrm.org/proxy/files/Events/2016/05%20May/Ulrich%20emerging%20trends%20in%20HR%202per(1).pdf

22. Tartell, Ph. D, Ross. "Aligning Training With Business Strategy." Training Magazine. N.p., 15 Nov. 2016. Web. 13 July 2017.

Chapter 5

1. Leib, S. (1991). *Principles of adult learning.* Retrieved from http://carrie-ekey.com/handouts/Rotterdam2012/Eu_Coaches_Conf2_Rott_Day_1_A4.pdf

2. Buskist, W., &Saville, B. K. (2001, March). Rapport-building: Creating positive emotional contexts for enhancing teaching and learning. *APSObserver, 14*(3). Retrieved from http://www.psychologicalscience.org/observer/0301/tips.html

Chapter 6

1. Mayer, R. E. (2011, December 1). On the role and design of video for learning. Retrieved from https://www. youtube.com/watch?v=S3fYg6OuTIA

2.   Bell, M. C., Kawadri, N., Simone, P. M., &Wiseheart, M. (2013). Long-term memory, sleep, and the spacing effect. *Memory, 22*(3), 276–83. Retrieved from https://www. researchgate.net/publication/236073229_Long-term_ memory_sleep_and_the_spacing_ effect

3.   L. Roediger, H. & A. Thorpe, L. Memory & Cognition (1978) 6: 296. doi: 10.3758/ BF03197459

Chapter 7

1.   Walsh, J. A., &Sattes, B. D. (2015). *Questioning for classroom discussion: Purposeful speaking, engaged listening, deep thinking.* Alexandria, VA: Association for Supervision & Curriculum Development.

2.   Ibid.

3.   Wheatley, M. J. (2002, April). It's an interconnected world. *Shambhala Sun.* Retrieved from http:// margaretwheatley.com/articles/interconnected.html

4.   Mazur, E. (1996). *Peer instruction: A user's manual.* Harlow, Essex: Pearson.

Chapter 8

1.   Grand View Research. (2017). *System integration market analysis by services (infrastructure & application integration, consulting), by end-use (IT & telecom, BFSI, healthcare, defense & security, retail, oil & gas), by region, & segment forecast, 2014–2015.* San Francisco, CA. Retrieved from http://www.grandviewresearch.com/industry-analysis/system-integration-market

2.   Markets and Markets. (2016). *System integration market worth 387.85 billion USD by 2021* [Press release]. Retrieved from http://www.marketsandmarkets.com/ PressReleases /system-integration.asp

3.   What is the Experience API? (n.d.). Retrieved from http://experienceapi.com/overview/

Chapter 9

1.   Dockweiler, S. (2014, October 15). *How much time do we spend in meetings? (Hint: It's scary).* Retrieved from https://www.themuse.com/advice/how-much-time-do-we-spend-in-meetings-hint-its-scary

2.   Tufte, E. (n.d.). *PowerPoint does rocket science—and better techniques for technical reports.* Retrieved from https://www.edwardtufte.com/bboard/q-and-a-fetch-msg?msg_id=0001yB

3.   Neill, C. (2012, November 30). *Amazon staff meetings: "No Powerpoint."* Retrieved from https:// conorneill.com/2012/11/30/amazon-staff-meetings-no-powerpoint/

Chapter 10

1.   Ho, C. (2015, February 23). Lawyers, could you pass this test? *The Washington Post.* Retrieved from https://www. highbeam.com/doc/1P2-37702170.html

Chapter 11

1.   Quinn, C. (2014, June 3). *Flipping Technology.* Retrieved from https://www.td.org/Publications/Blogs/ Learning-Technologies-Blog/2014/06/Flipping-Technology

2.   Gill, S. J. (2015, June 20). Pull, don't push, employee learning [Blog post]. Retrieved from http://stephenjgill.typepad.com/performance_ improvement_b/2015/06/pull-dont-push-employee-learning. html

3.   Grebow, D. (2015, June 19). The Internet of things that help you learn [Blog post]. Retrieved from https:// knowledgestarblog.wordpress.com/2015/06/19/the-internet-of-things-that-help-you-learn/

4.   Gill, S. J. (2015, February 12). Training culture vs. learning culture [Blog post]. Retrieved from http://stephenjgill.typepad.com/performance_ improvement_b/2015/02/training-culture-vs-learning-culture. html

5.   Gill, S. J. (2017, February 27). Reprise: The self-directed learner [Blog post]. Retrieved from http://stephenjgill.typepad.com/performance_ improvement_b/2017/02/reprise-the-self-directed-learner-. html

6.   Gill, S. J., &Grebow, D. (2017, January 25). The future of learning is not training [Blog post]. Retrieved from https://knowledgestarblog.wordpress.com/2017/01/25/the-future-of-learning-is-not-training/

7.   Pradhan, Arun. (2016, January 11). 5 reasons why 70:20:10 solutions fail (and what we can do about it) [Blog post]. Retrieved from http://design4performance. com/2016/01/11/5-reasons-why-702010-fails/

8.   Pradhan, Arun. (2016, June 14). Infographic: Work is learning [Blog post]. Retrieved from http://design4performance.com/category/learning-future/

9.   Pradhan, Arun. (2016, January 11). 5 reasons why 70:20:10 solutions fail (and what we can do about it) [Blog post]. Retrieved from http://design4performance.com/2016/01/11/5-reasons-why-702010-fails/

10.   Jennings, C. (2017, May 10). The knowledge and learning transfer problem [Blog post]. Retrieved from https://702010institute.com/knowledge-learning-transfer-problem/

11.   Mosher, B. (2017, March 9). *Compliance training: Cheers or jeers?* Retrieved from http://www.clomedia.com/2017/03/09/compliance-training-cheers-jeers/

12.   Gottfredson, C. (2012, June 18). Are you meeting all five moments of learning need? *Learning Solutions Magazine.* Retrieved from https://www.learningsolutionsmag.com/articles/949/are-you-meeting-all-five-moments-of-learning-need

13.   Masie, E. (n.d.). *OJL & performance support LAB.* Retrieved from https://masie.com/OJL/content.html

14.   Hilton, H. (2017, February 21). *Microlearning: What it is and what it isn't.* Retrieved from http://www.bottomlineperformance.com/microlearning-what-it-is-what-it-isnt/

Cross, J. (n.d.). Informal learning: Rediscovering the natural pathways that inspire innovation and performance [Blog post]. Retrieved from http://www.inforrnl.com/the-informal-learning-page/

Ordering Information

To order additional copies of

Flipped Learning 3.0
The Operating System for the
Future of Talent Development

Or to inquire about

Speeches, Seminars, and Workshops

Contact us at

www.flglobal.org

admin@flglobal.org

Made in the USA
Lexington, KY
21 September 2017